# GREEN MOUNTAINS

By the same author

# SAMARKAND
# BLACK SEA
# RED SANDS
# COLD KITCHEN

Praise for *Black Sea* and *Red Sands*:

'Her prose at its best reminds me of Lawrence Durrell's travel writing: taut, colorful, opinionated and full of zest.'

**Edward Lee, author of *Buttermilk Graffiti***

'She captures people, history, and the ineffable soul of cities with astonishing, almost novelistic precision... I can't remember any cookbook that's drawn me in quite like this.'

**Helen Rosner, Art of Eating judge**

'Eden writes beautifully, not just about food... but about what it means to live an unchanging way of life in a fast-changing world.'

**Bee Wilson, *The Sunday Times***

'Eden's blazing talent and unabashedly greedy curiosity will have you strapped in beside her...'

**Christine Muhlke, *The New York Times***

'There is nobody writing about food at the moment who's committed to this level of immersion and it rings out in every line.'

**Tim Hayward, *Financial Times***

'She has rightly won awards for her remarkable talent for telling stories that take the reader right to the heart of her experiences.'

**Lisa Markwell, *Sunday Times Magazine***

# GREEN MOUNTAINS

Walking the Caucasus with Recipes

## CAROLINE EDEN

Quadrille

Quadrille,
Penguin Random House UK,
One Embassy Gardens,
8 Viaduct Gardens, London SW11 7BW

Quadrille Publishing Limited is part of the
Penguin Random House group of companies
whose addresses can be found at global.
penguinrandomhouse.com

Text © Caroline Eden 2025
Food photography © Ola O. Smit 2025
Location photography © Caroline Eden
2025 with the exceptions of pages 6–7
© Matthieu Paley; 10–11 and 16–17 © Yulia
Grigoryants; 22 © Artem Darkov/Unsplash;
32 © Fifg/Alamy; 35 © istock; 42–43 and 45 ©
Matthieu Paley; 82 © Anna Sorokina/Stocksy;
96–97 © Mauritius Images/Alamy; 124 © Hemis/
Alamy; 133, 136, 140–141, 144–145 and 152–153
© Anush Babajanyan; 154 and 202 © Aaron
Huey; 207 © Thomas Pickard/Stocksy; 210–211 ©
Tomas Malik/Unsplash; 237 © Robert Harding/
Alamy; 242 © Marishka Tsiklauri/Unsplash; 256–
257 © Marita Kavelashvili/Unsplash; 266–267 ©
Ani Adigyozalyan/Unsplash; 280–281 © Savelie
Antipov/Unsplash
Illustration © Ivana Zorn 2025
Design and layout © Quadrille 2025

Caroline Eden has asserted her right to be
identified as the author of this Work in accordance
with the Copyright, Designs and Patents Act 1988

Published by Quadrille in 2025

www.penguin.co.uk

A CIP catalogue record for this book is available
from the British Library

ISBN 9781787138513
10 9 8 7 6 5 4 3 2 1

Printed in Estonia by PrintBest
Colour reproduction by F1

The authorised representative in the EEA is Penguin
Random House Ireland, Morrison Chambers, 32
Nassau Street, Dublin D02 YH68.

Managing Director Sarah Lavelle
Senior Commissioning Editor Stacey Cleworth
Project Editor Sofie Shearman
Designer Dave Brown
Design Manager Katherine Case
Food Photographer Ola O. Smit
Location Photographers Caroline Eden
Image Researcher Liz Boyd
Illustration Ivana Zorn
Props Stylist Tabitha Hawkins
Food Stylist Holly Cowgill
Food Stylist Assistant Lucy Cottle
Head of Production Stephen Lang
Production Controller Martina Georgieva

With thanks to the Sevan Writers' House, the Gallery
of Mariam and Eranuhi Aslamazyan Sisters and the
Parajanov Museum.

'O, who can hold a fire in his hand
By thinking on the frosty Caucasus?
Or cloy the hungry edge of appetite
By bare imagination of a feast?'

– William Shakespeare (*Richard II*)


'I have cultivated in myself a sixth sense,
an "Ararat" sense: the sense of attraction
to a mountain.'

– Osip Mandelstam (*Journey to Armenia*)

To James and for the hospitable people of Armenia and Georgia,

who so often go out of their way to help a stranger.

# CONTENTS

# PRELUDE AND SETTING

*Tomorrow, that horizon, that hill. Push on. Keep on pushing.*

Like a cook, a hill walker is not born but made. Just as no one starts off in the kitchen as a pastry chef, nobody climbs a mountain before they've walked countless miles. That much is obvious. But less apparent are the parallels between the two eternal human routines of cooking and walking. Both are physical pursuits combining the emotional with the practical and, nowadays, when the preparation of food is not always drudgery, and walking not always a task, both can offer salvation.

Follow the steps of a recipe and become satisfied. Go outside, walk about and relish being among changing scenery and fresh air. Put one foot in front of the other, or place food you've made on the table, and feel, in return, contentment, maybe even a certain calmness and relief. What at first seems daunting, becomes, through practice and over time, an activity often anticipated and savoured. Good for the body, good for the soul. Cooking and walking can be reliable methods for gathering up enough strength and sanity to keep going during troubled times. And what troubled times these are.

Since Russia's full-scale invasion of Ukraine, much has changed within the countries, and communities, featured in my previous books in this trilogy, *Black Sea* and *Red Sands*, stretching from eastern Europe to Central Asia. In fact, since I began working on this third and final instalment, *Green Mountains*, you could say that everything has changed.

Russia's brutal war against Ukraine capsized the entire Black Sea region but it has impacted Central Asia, too, the focus of *Red Sands*. Many families there, especially in Tajikistan and Kyrgyzstan, who rely on relatives sending home money from jobs in Russia, are suffering from the unstable rouble. And the Russian army has been targeting Central Asia for recruits. This is an affront to the Central Asian countries, whose leaders are generally against the war, and whose governments have launched campaigns to warn their citizens of such manoeuvres as well as outlawing fighting for Russia.

Across the Caspian Sea, where *Red Sands* began, in the South Caucasus, a myriad of different challenges has been unfolding as well.

In Georgia, tensions have been at a tipping point since tens of thousands of Russians fleeing mobilisation arrived, no visa required. After the full-scale invasion of Ukraine, their convergence on the capital, Tbilisi (population: 1.1 million), has meant surging rents and walls covered with angry anti-Russian graffiti. Many Georgians see the Kremlin's invasion of their country, 15 years ago, the wounds still raw, as one of the foundations for its attacks on Ukraine. On Batumi's Black Sea boulevard, in southwestern Georgia, it is often Russian, not Georgian, that is heard most commonly, so large are the numbers of arrivals. With resentment melding with fear, some Georgians have been appealing to impose a visa regime for those crossing the border. It is a very uneasy balance.

Armenia also found itself a favoured destination for Russian exiles. But there the prime minister, Nikol Pashinyan, was busy dealing with other fraught issues. He accused the Kremlin of failing its peacekeeper duties by ignoring the Azerbaijani ambition to ethnically cleanse Nagorno-Karabakh (an Armenian majority 'island' in the region of Azerbaijan known to Armenians as Artsakh) of Armenians, a claim Baku denies. In the course of writing this book, much to the horror of Armenia, Azerbaijan's lightning offensive triggered the rapid, and traumatic, exodus of almost all ethnic Armenians, ending their centuries-long existence there.

A new edition of *Black Sea* was published in the autumn of 2023, and in it I explored the role of the sea in the war, how Russians are transiting stolen grain from Ukraine and how Odesa, defiant against shelling and blackouts, has gained UNESCO protection. Also, how across the border in Turkey, the Bosphorus continues to be a flashpoint of Russia's ongoing war against Ukraine, one of warships, grain deals, smuggling and espionage.

### LANDS BETWEEN THE SEAS

Given this tortured state of affairs, it is natural, I think, to turn to the outdoors and, if you are able, to employ the art of walking not as a way of ignoring such huge events and terrible hostilities, but to use it as a means to try to process the circumstances. And, in turn, to feel the benefits of walking's common cure. As the polar explorer Apsley Cherry-Garrard once urged: 'take that man out-of-doors and walk him about: Nature will do the rest.'

In *Black Sea* and *Red Sands*, I covered thousands of miles and many countries, almost all of it overland, by train, bus and car. For this book, I wanted to slow right down and to do what I could by foot. And, I wanted the region covered to be the lands between the Black Sea, the topic of my first book, and the Caspian Sea where the second book, *Red Sands*, began. The Caucasus therefore. Familiar territory but fresh ground.

But which direction for the compass? Where to start? With walking, firstly it is necessary to pick a rough route. In that regard, it is simple.

When I first began thinking of this book, back in 2019, I'd planned to complete the journey in Dagestan, in the North Caucasus, one of seven autonomous republics in southern Russia, but the war put that firmly out of range. Putin's Russia had become not only a thoroughly immoral destination to visit, but a dangerous one, too. I had wanted to go in order to taste the village flatbreads that I'd heard are sometimes still pricked in the traditional way with goose feather quills and I'd hoped, also, to try the legendary khinkal – pouch-like dumplings made with kefir dough, which are similar to but different from the more famous Georgian khinkali – and to see the drying of meats in autumn when seasonally it is warm but insects are fewer. But that would have to wait, maybe even for another lifetime.

Therefore, *Green Mountains* focuses on the South Caucasus, a landscape of clefted valleys and ancient cities. By beginning beneath the Lesser Caucasus range in Armenia, I chose a direction that would gradually move northwards, up to Georgia and to the shadows of the Greater Caucasus, before ending up on the Black Sea where it all began.

But this, too, is an area riven by complex antagonisms and geopolitics. My chosen route meant leaving out neighbouring Azerbaijan, also a place of emerald-green mountains, fascinating food (a book ought to be written on the wildly varied pilafs alone), convivial villages and compelling stories. But given the current conflict with Armenia, including both countries in one book, for now at least, felt misguided.

That is the route, then. But what of the quest?

As an outsider, by walking, you immediately become part of the scenery. By not shutting yourself away from the world, in the body of a car or bus, you make yourself vulnerable, approachable and more open to encounters. You have to face whatever you walk into, good and bad.

Therefore, walking offers the best chance to relish the smells, sights and tastes, all of the sensory things that make up the fabric of a place. By hopefully stepping out, and by putting my trust in walking, I had faith that a certain human, animal, botanical, and edible portrait of Armenia and Georgia would form. Whether

walking into mountain valleys, or through towns and cities, I'd carry with me confidence in the path ahead, and optimism for the weather, the map and good health. To paraphrase the writer Iain Sinclair, who famously tramped London's peripheries: walking sews it all together.

## FOOTSTEPS TO FLAVOURS

Food is woven through these on-foot adventures because of a very simple idea: the fact that no meal – *literally no meal* – can compete with what is served to you after a long walk. The deep, primeval happiness and comfort that comes from a bowl of beans or soup or roasted meat or grilled fish that arrives at the table where you have finally sat down, is one of the very most satisfying and pleasurable things in life.

First, there is the immediate gratitude for the easing of hunger. Then there is relief as carbohydrates, protein and calories provide the goodness that will aid recovery, and then, just as importantly, there is the connection to the surrounding landscape: you might eat meat or vegetables from the nearby land, fruit and nuts from the adjacent orchard, maybe fish from the local rivers. And there is the bond, too, the relationship with your host who is feeding you, and the thankfulness you feel towards them. The straightforward, yet intense, pleasure of eating hard-earned food that has been thoughtfully prepared by a cook. A happy exchange. Footsteps to flavours, travelling towards sustenance. A moment when even the most rudimentary of meals becomes a satisfying and cherished banquet. Yes, the post-walk meal, and all the physical and emotional factors that come with it, is something that truly does make life, even at the hardest junctures, worth living for.

And where better in the world to test this uncomplicated philosophy than Armenia and Georgia? Not only do both countries offer world-class hiking but the cult of the kitchen exists absolutely everywhere. These are lands where the cook's hands are gifted with abundance: ancient wheat varieties, gardens filled with mandarins, gorges tangled with wild unknowable herbs and sheep in the valleys. Wineries to rival any you can name. The moreish juice of sweet grapes and yellow plums, the soft flesh of strawberries and apricots suspended in jam. Magical cheeses. Mountain summertime greens that have no name in English as they grow only there. The coastline, in Georgia, is an open-air Black Sea hothouse bursting with citrus, tea, tobacco, bamboo, cork trees and eucalyptus. And far and wide, all manner of things are busily minced and cubed and stuffed and ground and pitted and dried in the sun to be preserved for winter. These are the lands where, a local proverb goes, 'A man only has to spit on the ground for an orange to grow.'

Similarities, and differences, between the cuisines of these neighbouring countries, quickly appeared. Both have exceedingly good bread, mineral waters, dairy and fruit. Both have a strong focus on fresh herbs, spices and a genuine attention to seasonality. The Syrian and Lebanese influence on Armenia's restaurant scene – brought about by the arrival of ethnic Armenians from those countries – was less known to me before arriving, and it was greatly appealing. And while Georgia's wine industry is far more developed, Armenia also has stupendous wines, ready to be more widely discovered. Anyone in doubt of the Georgian commitment to wine should look up the work of ethnographer Giorgi Chitaia, who viewed viticulture in Georgia as a source of life: the harvesting of grapes a communal holiday, the crushing of them a sacred act. 'The juice from the first crush – pure wine – is set aside and dedicated to the glory of St. George', he once said.

The crop of recipes I have included here, or as I like to call them, edible postcards, are a way for me, a home cook, to send something of the flavours of Armenia and Georgia onwards to you. Though not perfect, or strictly authentic, they were all crafted out of curiosity and affection, and with a huge admiration for the cooks who fed me so well throughout my journeys. At the end of every single walk, without exception, there would always be the opportunity for good food, and often excellent wine, carefully prepared.

## MAESTROS, MAVERICKS AND MOUNTAINEERS

It is a region, too, to feast upon psychologically: through film, literature, art and the journals and photographs of great alpinists born in the vertical villages of the Caucasus. Writers have long turned to these countries for inspiration. Novelist and war reporter, Vasily Grossman (born in Berdychiv, Ukraine), found solace by Armenia's Lake Sevan while censored by the KGB, and went on to write *An Armenian Sketchbook*. The poet Osip Mandelstam (born in Warsaw in 1891 and raised in St Petersburg) visited Armenia for several months in 1930, before he was targeted by the Soviet authorities. Of clouds swirling about Mount Ararat he wrote: 'It was the descending–ascending motion of cream poured into a glass of ruddy tea, dispersing in all directions like curly-puffed tubers.' Mount Ararat is today cut off from Armenia, just over the border in Turkey, but at over 5,000 metres it is, depending on the weather, visible from the capital, Yerevan. John Steinbeck fell in love with Georgia while there with the war photographer Robert Capa, and their experiences were recorded in *A Russian Journal*, published in 1948. We will meet these writers during the journeys recounted here.

Maestro and filmmaker of the Caucasus, Sergei Parajanov, is best remembered for his luxurious and confounding film *The Colour of Pomegranates*, and we will delve into his masterpieces with an expert curator in Yerevan. Staying in Armenia, we will also explore the work of Mariam and Yeranuhi Aslamazyan, two Armenian sisters, who painted dynamic still lifes of the fruits and vegetables of their homeland, often

from afar. Mountaineers, their lives and legacies, form an important part of the cultural jigsaw, so we'll also meet several renowned climbers including Mikhail Khergiani, 'the tiger of the cliffs', and Guram Tikanadze, who scaled the highest peaks of the Caucasus, as well as Joyce Dunsheath, a quietly intrepid English woman who secured a hard-to-get permit to climb the greatest mountains of the Caucasus during the closed-off Soviet era.

## AND THE COLOUR GREEN?

Green is the colour of the Caucasus Mountains in summertime. The season when the blooming hillsides, generously warmed by the sun, are places of foraging, exploring and shepherding. Sublime and inviting. A green topcoat for a richly fertile landscape and its soil that nourishes hornbeam, pine, fir, hawthorn, medlar, Persian walnut, chestnut, wild pear, apple and cherry plum trees.

When far away from the Caucasus, but dreaming of those lofty crags and rolling elevations, to me they are always green, green, green. Dizzyingly green.

It is the green of summer that, of course, best encourages walking: to frontiers, to meet highlanders, to explore the polyphonic tapestries of different communities. A colour that fires up the road and picnics, and encourages seasonal inns and taverns to open their doors. Green hills and budding leaves, that coax walkers out to feel the heartbeats of cities, or onwards to travel deeper into the cradle of Christianity: to monasteries, hermitages, churches and ancient villages. Whatever the season, though, this is an unpredictable terrain, mired by famously fickle mountain weather, that can make for testing hikes. But equally it has never been more accessible with new technology, improved mapping and trails constantly opening up.

Travellers willing to make the journey have long known the special sort of generosity that awaits. Herodotus commented favourably on the Armenians as innkeepers, Xenophon wrote of the appalling cold, but also of benevolence. And therefore it is true that when walking among such a geography, that is not only enchanting but inhabited by such open-handed and open-hearted people, one of the most difficult things is knowing when to stop. There is a constant and potently persuasive urge to just go beyond that valley, to see that particular mountain, that church, that village. These are green mountains capable of transforming almost anybody into a pilgrim.

– Edinburgh, 2024

# PART ONE

# ARMENIA

# TROUBLE IN THE VALLEY OF WOES

If an Armenian hands you an apricot they are, in a way, handing you Armenia. It is the flavour of summer, fruit of health, symbol of life, badge of the country and emblem of the people.

*Prunus armeniaca* is the fruit's Latin name, hinting at its native origins. Fifty varieties grow in Armenia and 6,000-year-old apricot stones have been dug up from the country's soil. One band of Armenia's tricolour flag is apricot-hued and Yerevan's international film festival is named the Golden Apricot. Impressions of the fuzzy-skinned fruit beautify postage stamps and aged apricot wood is carved into the duduk, the oboe-like instrument which forms the melancholic sound of Armenia, the musical notes of the performer giving life again to the tree, and its fruit. It is, therefore, a gift of great meaning.

So, when a hand, stained amber from motor oil, reached in through the open window of the car I was sitting in and gently tipped not one but four apricots from his fist into my palm, they felt like a prize. A wordless bestowal from one stranger to another. An act of unexpected kindness.

*A sign or token, a trophy or edible medal?* I wondered silently. Because that same afternoon, my husband James and I thought that we were going to die: out there, somewhere on a sizzlingly hot, frighteningly remote mountain plateau in southeastern Armenia in the province of Vayots Dzor, also known as the 'Valley of Woes' because of the countless calamitous earthquakes that have shaken its canyons. Armenia, sitting where the Arabian tectonic plate grinds against the Eurasian one, is prone to convulsions. The country has been torn apart by seismic waves many times, the worst in recent history being the 1988 Spitak earthquake which shattered the northwest, killing tens of thousands. While it wasn't a tremor that had made me shake with fear, it was something borne of nature, less dramatic but just as capable of killing should you be in the wrong place when it randomly hits.

Smiling, the stranger walked away, returning to his petrol pump on the side of a road busy with trucks spinning up dust. I watched him go, his hands now empty and tucked into the pockets of his overalls. Putting the apricots in a neat row on the dashboard, my chest and clothes still wet with sweat, I wanted to preserve them, there and then, as a memento of my near-death experience.

I sat completely still, relishing the calm, as James paid for the petrol. Across the street, Armenia's wine sat warming up to the temperature of hot tea in plastic Coca-Cola bottles to be picked up by Iranian truckers who bought it, disguised, to carry home to Iran where alcohol is banned but the market for illegal wine

is thriving. I pictured the Silk Road city of Tabriz, across the Armenian–Iranian border, just a few hours' drive away, with its bazaars of coppersmiths and carpets.

Matching the rose-pink, desert-sand colour of the sunset painting the valley, the apricots wobbled and rocked gently as we drove off. I stared at them feeling numb, the very last of the adrenalin draining away.

## CINNAMON CANYONS AND BLUE POPPIES

The walk had started promisingly. Vayots Dzor, as well as being the least-populated province of Armenia, famous for its dramatic mountain landscapes, is also home to the country's best-known monastery, Noravank, and the spa town of Jermuk, namesake of the madly popular local brand of mineral water. And there are ancient winemaking traditions, too, focused on the indigenous dark and complex Areni grape, known to everyone as 'Areni Noir'. A strong set of credentials and therefore a natural southern starting point.

Perilously high temperatures were forecast but we were prepared: hats on, arms and legs covered. Rucksacks loaded with six litres of water, plus compass, walking maps and a picnic that Mary, the cook at the guesthouse, had made for us. We'd set off sensibly early from the regional capital, Yeghegnadzor, two hours southeast of the capital Yerevan, keen to get ahead of the devilish sun. 'Back in time for dinner,' we'd assured Mary, who, in turn, had promised us arishta, ribbon-like Armenian pasta, and herby salads from her kitchen garden.

At the starting point on the map, not far from the village of Gomk (population: 162), we parked our rented three-door Lada Niva, white, boxy as an ambulance and almost unchanged since it first rolled off the Russian assembly line in 1977, alongside two fluffy calves by a farm in Kapuyt (population: 23).

The livestock trail was shady and green, offering ample cover to keep the car cool and, as we turned the engine off, a shepherd appeared from around the corner of a dry-stone wall nodding at us that it was okay to park, that we were welcome. Out of the car, checking at least twice that we had everything, I stretched and stepped out into a strong, but not unpleasant, smell of cow pats, dozens of them scattered on the dirt track like giant chocolate chip cookies.

We began climbing. Following a rough path in the direction of a canyon we trod on parched ground, dusty and stony, which soon became overgrown with brush and long grass up to our knees. Despite trousers, this meant an urgent change of walking style. Tap, tap, tap, went our walking poles, hitting the ground hard with each stride. An unnatural tactic but a crucial one, acting as a warning signal for snakes. Armenia's snakes – over twenty different species – are countless in the hot south where ready access to any anti-venom is uncertain. Fear of them, slinking silently through the undergrowth, had inscribed their names on my brain: there is the dwarf snake (breeds in summer, hunts spiders and small lizards at twilight), the coin-marked Asian racer (harmless) and the Armenian viper (highly venomous).

The sun struck murderously down as we went lumbering on, higher and higher, zigzagging up the hillside, following the scrubby way the map suggested not far from where a minor branch of the Silk Road was said to have once stretched. Our aim was the top where a plateau would open up offering tremendous vistas and, with the higher altitude and flat ground, fresher air and ease of walking. Tiring as it was, we had not expected the way to be easy. Vayots Dzor is mountain country; there is Mount Vardenis (3,522 metres), the volcanic Vayots Sar (2,581 metres) and Mount Gandzak (2,374 metres).

It was far too hot to speak so we quietly pushed on with every breath pulled in requiring effort. Other than the buzzing of insects, all was hushed, strangely so.

A little higher up we were met with dozens of traffic cone-like ant hills and some of the insects escaped their colonies, hitching a ride on our legs. The views, buff-coloured escarpments mixed with surprisingly green slopes, were uninterrupted by anything man-made as far as the eye could see. But while there was no sign of people, my guidebook mentioned rock hieroglyphs not far away, showing hunting scenes that prove a long history of human habitation.

Shelving fears of snakes, I began picking out plants I recognised: hardy knapweed and familiar cow parsley growing freely all around, with snowy-headed yarrow and ox-eye daisies springing up between rocks and basket-of-gold with its grey-green leaves and its golden flowers imitating the sun's mustard-hued rays.

Every thirty minutes or so we stopped to drink. We knew the trek would take about four to five hours, covering just 15 kilometres, quite short but painfully steep, so we rationed the water carefully. Sweat poured in quick rivulets, soaking my neck, back and head until my shoulder-length hair became a dripping scarf that maddened me.

'I think we've gone wrong,' James said, mouthing the words you never want to hear on a walk.

And with that, having hacked a couple of kilometres through scrubby, arm-scratching knee-high bushes, we backtracked, to only go up again at a slightly different angle, all the way dive-bombed by a cloud of droning summer flies. The path, increasingly steep and narrow, meant we progressed very slowly,

choosing footholds amidst the small sharp jutting rocks and avoiding the hollows filled with spiky bushes and crumbling, slippery soil leading to the valley far below. At one bend, a little shade, and a little wind to keep the insects at bay. Exhausted, we stopped for the picnic that Mary had prepared for us. Garden herbs of parsley, dill and tarragon were enclosed in thin lavash, the bread that forms the backbone of Armenia's diet, with a little brined white cheese and there were foil-wrapped roast potatoes and whole stubby cucumbers that we gnawed on thirstily. Breath and composure recovered, I told James about the ancient Copper Age cowhide shoe I'd read about.

In 2008, a 'trekh' shoe was found here by archaeologists led by a team from Cork, Ireland. A woman's lace-up, it is one of the oldest, if not *the* oldest shoe in the world, believed to be 5,500 years old (similar-aged shoes have been found in graves in Israel). Among the finds in the same cave, known as Areni-1, not far from where we were walking, was also a 6,000-year-old human brain, a deer's shoulder blade, fish vertebra and evidence of a 6,100-year-old winery where wine was likely produced for burial ceremonies.

'Come on, we have to keep going,' said James, bored of the shoe story and never one to stop for too long. Dusting ourselves off we carried on walking in single file, focusing on this beast of a hike.

After a couple of sweltering hours, again whacking through scrub with our walking poles, we slouched up to the very top, the last metres feeling all but impossible. The undergrowth was so thick and the way so steep that I began hallucinating bottles of icy beer. But eventually, we made it. Horizontal ground was a blessed relief, like no other, and my limbs trembled from the exertion. Views of the cinnamon-hued canyon began opening up like a picture book. Green, green ridges and bluffs met huge copper-coloured gullies and grey ravines. Huge lonely gorges. The air was fizzy and soft-focused with the heat rising from the earth in waves. Red and blue poppies nodded in the breeze.

With faces the colour of magenta, we sighed and sighed, and drank it all in, slowing down to enjoy the release of walking on level ground, refusing the temptation to grumble about weariness. Blissfully cut off from the world, and with a little breeze buffeting welcomingly, it felt wonderful to be on the top, to triumphantly stride across the grassy highland. Hearts pulsing a little slower, finally. The view was utterly unhindered. No roads, no pylons in the distance, no houses or people. But that respite, that ease, so hard fought for, vanished in less than half an hour.

First it was a switch in the atmosphere. A heaviness in the air and an unearthly light all around, silvery and brooding and unnatural for the hour, like twilight come early. Then, in quick succession, a distinct headache-inducing oppressiveness and the unmistakable sound of crackling thunderclaps in the distance.

'We need to get off of here, and quickly,' James warned.

Sweat still stinging my dusty face, I was exhausted and finally, enjoying the reward of climbing up for hours. Going down would be just as hard as coming up, especially at speed. Hard on the knees. I had been relishing the idea of descending slowly – especially as we had ample daylight left.

For a few minutes, the valley was still again and I thought maybe we'd gotten away with it. But then the booming came back, stronger and closer. Pressure buzzing violently in the air.

'When thunder roars, go indoors,' I said, idiotically.

'Quick, Caroline. This is serious. You need to speed up. We are totally exposed up here.'

Taking fire at those words, I started jogging jerkily in my heavy leather snake-resistant walking boots.

Unused to violent summer storms, or loud noises generally among hills (except for the roar of a stag in the Scottish Highlands), or the need to hurry quite so much on a hillwalk, the urgency felt unnatural. But the storm coming over the mountains was real and directly upon us and the savagery of the thunder came closer and closer, tighter and tighter, surrounding us like a noose. Demonic flashes followed. Vivid violet glares, one bolt after the next thrown down like the silvery wands of a mountain magician. The land lit up, the ground shook.

*Was this really happening?* It was.

Very quickly, the lightning strikes got closer. Like shooting stars and comets hurled down from the gods, looking for something to hit. Biblical weather. God's displeasure. The world no longer felt known, but weird. Images of Frankenstein flashed through my mind and of violent rupturing earthquakes, the very phenomena that formed the Caucasus mountain ranges millions of years ago. I ran on, remembering how I'd watched a similar storm break over the South China Sea once, from the safety of a large boat far away, how different that

31

had been as I sat alone at night on the deck, feet up, sipping a beer, watching the lightning fork down, viewing it as an exciting spectacle not something to fear.

Every second felt like a minute and I trembled weakly with each furious bolt. It was like being shot at by a drunken marksman. A horrible cold pulse crept up and down my spine.

'Get down, lay on the ground. We need to be low ...' said James as the rest of his words were lost to another tremendous clap of thunder.

Cowering, I flattened myself to the earth, flinching at every flash and its accompanying blast. Each thunder roar was like an avalanche tumbling down. Damp hair now matted with dust, blood pulsing hard in my ears with the terrified anticipation of what might follow, I concentrated on breathing, each gasp pronounced, while true fear hastened up from the gut. James threw our metal trekking poles, surely a deadly magnet, far away.

*This could be the end of us.*

The warm dirt smelled faintly of toasted cumin and with my face upon it, I began minutely examining my surroundings. Ants. Grass. Beetles, small and black with red polka dots. I thought of the Hittite storm gods I'd seen in museums across the border in Turkey. *No wonder humans felt a need to placate them*, I thought. I shut my eyes, then when I opened them, I saw a bolt hit the ground less than twenty metres away. I felt an intense wave of depletion, which is how helplessness feels.

*What a way to go, fried by lightning up here. Who would find us? And when?*

Nature was shattered and alarmed: birds had fallen silent, the light was a sickly yellow. A field mouse, emboldened by fright, brushed right past my arm, running scared. I started to pray under my breath, tongue sticking to the roof of my mouth.

'We need to run, we can't stay here. We need to get off this hill. Now!'

James grabbed my hand as we jumped up and started running.

Terror made us solar-powered, and we sprinted down the mountain like gundogs. Thankfully the route was far less overgrown than the way we'd come up and so we went spiralling along, trying not to skid over, as the land lit up again and again with wild flashes. Down and down and further down, hugging any rocks we passed for momentary cover. Finally, terraced meadows of the plains came into view and with them stables and huts, signs of habitation.

As we reached the bottom, the storm passed us, with the thunder rolling further then further away and the lightning stopping. My legs wobbled, my heart pounded. What terrible timing we had to be at the top just as it peaked.

When our hired car came into sight, it was one of the best things I had ever seen. We sat still for a moment, resting, heated faces flushed with sweat. Then the land came alive again, birdsong returned, flies soared out of their shelters, the two calves we'd seen earlier came around a corner towards us. But there was still no rain other than a few teasing drops. No cool respite or the delicious smell of wet earth.

Coated in dirt, we returned to the guesthouse and, carrying the four petrol station apricots, I walked straight into the kitchen, breathing in the rich and lovely smells of fats, herbs, cheese and wine, to tell Mary, partly using sign language, what had happened. She gasped and laughed but didn't seem that surprised.

We washed with ample hot water and composed ourselves on the small wooden balcony of our bedroom, still amazed, and horrified, by the novelty of our situation earlier. The guesthouse felt like a true refuge. The owner, Gagik Sardaryan, a keen hiker himself, had used green-hued stone and wood to build the inn, echoing the outlook. When dinner was ready, Mary ushered us to a table and onto wicker chairs set right on the grass. Sloping downwards was the verdant pistachio-green kitchen garden with its abundant cucumbers, sorrel, apricots, green plums, tomatoes, beans, figs, yellow cherries, onions and more unfamiliar greens and medicinal plants. A corner of the garden was given over entirely to the cultivation of herbs. All was tranquil.

First came a carafe of heartsblood-coloured local wine, a jug of cherry kompot and a pitcher of sparkling Jermuk water with fresh tarragon blades bobbing in it, all of which raised spirits and calmed any remaining nerves. Relief, like a drug, washed over us and we sat in a kind of worn-out stupor, just as a huge Armenian moon began to rise, the colour of steel.

Soup, thick with bulgur and revitalising greens and summer herbs came next, then a spry garden salad, and the promised arishta pasta, served plain with a little butter, black pepper and oil. Afterwards, a rich dark chocolate cake, topped with fresh raspberries and mint leaves. Armenian brandy, drunk with sureness. There was even more to eat and drink than we had anticipated and we lingered over it all as no meal could have been better or more welcome. It felt like a miracle.

In the garden that night, under a sky black and quiet, we took out our phones and looked up what to do in the face of such tremendous weather, ashamed that we hadn't had this vital knowledge to call up earlier. Generally, the advice is to curl up into a tight ball, to make yourself as small as possible, not to lay flat as we did. I also learned, during my online research, that Nietzsche experienced bursts of creative energy during such storms and that two teenage sisters had been killed by lightning on a mountain somewhere in Scandinavia that same week.

I imagined huge dreams would await that night, how soft sleep would wrap up our exhausted bodies now that we'd feasted so well. Armenia, what a country! What a start to an adventure that was only just beginning.

# Mary's Kitchen Garden Soup

At the Green Stone Guesthouse, after surviving the intense lightning storm, we sat at a rickety wooden table, unsteady on grass, barefoot and not caring about ankle-biting insects. And under moonlight in this little oasis, when after this hydrating soup had been served, we indulged a long celebratory pause, paired with an Ararat Slim cigarette, then raised a toast: 'To life! We are alive, we are alive!' And as we did this, two young winemakers checked in, stripped off and jumped straight into the small garden swimming pool. Moonstruck, full of life and full of love.

**SERVES 4**

60g/2¼oz medium bulgur wheat

Sea salt and freshly ground black pepper

2 tbsp olive oil

1 red bell pepper, chopped

1 large onion, finely chopped

2 garlic cloves, finely chopped

2 tbsp tomato purée (paste)

¼ tsp cayenne pepper

¼ tsp sweet paprika

200g/7oz canned chopped tomatoes

700ml/3 cups chicken stock

½ teaspoon red wine vinegar

Generous handful of soft herbs (a mix of parsley, basil, dill, tarragon), chopped

200g/7oz mixed leafy summery greens (spinach, sorrel, rocket (arugula), lovage)

Juice of 1 lemon

Sumac (optional)

Put the bulgur into a saucepan and pour over enough boiling water to cover by 1cm/½in, then clamp on a lid, bring to the boil, turn down the heat and simmer for 15 minutes. Try a couple of grains to check if it is cooked – it should still have bite and texture. Season well with salt and pepper and set aside.

Heat the oil in a large casserole or saucepan over a medium heat and sauté the red pepper and onion, with salt and pepper, until soft, then add the garlic and stir until its pungency lessens. Add the tomato purée, stir well, then add the spices and cook for a couple of minutes. Next, add the chopped tomatoes, stock and vinegar and cook gently for 5 minutes.

Stir through the herbs, along with the greens and lemon juice, then check the seasoning and let the soup bubble for 5 minutes more.

Remove the soup from the heat, adding a little hot water if you find it too thick, and stir through the bulgur (only when ready to serve – it will go to mush if left in stock). Ladle into bowls and dust with sumac, if you wish.

# Trout Baked with Orange and Raspberry

As an early Christian nation, viticulture in Armenia is so ancient that Herodotus wrote of it being shipped to Babylon in the 5th century BCE and Xenophon, student of Socrates, noted the fragrant wines when marching through with his armies. Armenia doesn't (yet) have the same level of out-and-out wine obsession as Georgia, but it is a fast-developing scene. Close to the Green Stone Guesthouse is the Old Bridge Winery where one afternoon we feasted on an inventive dish of trout, not with tarragon as is most common in Armenia, but baked with orange and oregano, and served with a sharp raspberry sauce. The owner, Armen Khalatyan, recommended a bottle of dry red wine from the rocky vineyards close by, reminding us that when it comes to fish, wine does not always have to be white.

**SERVES 2**

2 small trout (roughly 350g/12oz each), gutted and cleaned but heads on

1 small orange, halved then sliced into thin half-moon crescents

115g/4oz fresh raspberries

1 tbsp olive oil

1 tbsp cider vinegar

Sea salt flakes and freshly ground black pepper

Handful of fresh oregano (or thyme) sprigs

Preheat the oven to 200°C/400°F/gas mark 6. Using a sharp knife, slash the fish no more than 1cm/½in deep, four times on each side. Push the orange slices into the slits. Place on a large baking tray lined with foil, leaving space between, and bring the sides of the foil up to wrap and seal the trout. Bake for 20 minutes.

While the trout cooks, blend the raspberries with the oil, vinegar, a pinch of salt and 1 tablespoon of water, then force through muslin or similar to remove the seeds.

Remove the fish from the oven and open the foil parcel. Sprinkle over some salt and pepper then scatter the oregano over and bake again, foil open this time, for 6 minutes or until the fish is cooked through. Serve with fresh bread and salad, along with the raspberry dressing.

# THE GOLDEN WAY TO NORAVANK

The day, newly minted and hot as a bread oven, began with coffee and birdsong on the brightly lit wooden balcony. We didn't want to leave the warm-hearted comforts of the Green Stone Guesthouse, full of good humour and Mary's excellent cooking, but we did. There was a zigzagging trail to tackle, high above the monastery of Noravank, and I'd heard a rumour of a good café, hidden in a cave, to finish up at. All the ingredients, therefore, of a gratifying walk, *if* we could find the café and *if* the walk would not be cut short by the heatwave or some other unexpected drama.

Back in the Lada, we headed southwest, driving for less than an hour on baked tracks before parking up at the start point. Built on a rocky ledge on the steep slopes of an unforgiving valley, Noravank Monastery matched the tobacco colour of its Utah-like surroundings. But that is not to say it was a stark dustbowl setting year-round, far from it. Tributaries of the Arpa River meander along it and after rainfall, during spring, the lower slopes turn emerald green and white with blossoming apricot trees. In the heat, it was harder to picture the heavy snow that cuts off the roads to Noravank come deep winter, and tricky, too, despite the visitors car park filling up with minibuses, to imagine a thriving café in such a parched and secluded environment.

Lacing up walking boots, and grabbing the walking poles, James and I began following a skinny trail, heaving our way through the insufferably hot canyon, tugged upwards by the promise of far-reaching views of the monastery complex. Everything visible wobbled in heatwaves, the sun itself seeming to multiply in the sky. One step at a time, necks prickling with sweat, we avowed a respect for the path and accepted that in such unreasonable heat it would be a slog, but that it was also a privilege to walk above such an ancient and lonesome site. Any pace felt too fast but with limited water, there wasn't an option to slacken too much. We kept on pushing forwards, the way looking as though it had never seen a drop of water. The surrounding ravine, too, a towering scorched patchwork of terracotta-hued rock, also appeared insupportable for life. But of course that isn't the case. There are yellow daisy-like flower heads of aromatic achillea, purple Oriental knight's spur and red scarlet stonecrop. Unseen are bezoar goats with impressive horns and cloven hooves that make light work of the hillsides. Just in view, far, far away in the midheavens, are vulture-like birds.

## SUN DOGS AND SUMMER HERBS

We carried on up the arduous track, one that would have been easy in the cool. When we'd hoisted ourselves up to a decent enough elevation, I allowed myself a pause, sucking in as much dry, hot air as possible, deep into my burning lungs. Squinting hard at the monastery across the valley, my eyes met dozens of caves dotting the ridges surrounding it, honeycomb caverns appearing as lookouts. Nests for bears. It was impossible, looking at these nooks, not to feel a sense of being watched.

Sun dogs appeared, those spots of light that sometimes pop up on either side of the sun, shining like halos. My eyes streamed as I scrunched them up, unused to such sun-soaked and heat-hazed vistas, wildly different from British weather, so often grey and foul. Following the signposts that the eco-tourism path-building organisation Barev Trails had erected, we pushed upwards, passing an abandoned school bus and the foundations of a deserted village. With no shade anywhere, the only relief to be had was the view of the holy monastery itself and the welcome sensuousness of wild thyme and minty scents that were breathing out across the valley like perfume.

Such heat threatens normal thinking and I did begin to feel peculiar quite quickly, despite drinking ample water. In such landscapes, that speak of desert purity and absolutism, there is often a drawing in, a wordless communication between the walker and the environment. Dry, dry ground, the dirt, dried leaves and gravel grinding and milling underfoot, each step sounding like a giant biting into a cracker. Spend too long in such an unforgiving environment and you run the risk of hallucinations. Eventually the rhythm of walking is relied upon for sanity, steps repeated and repeated again, necessary for switching off. Crunch, crunch, crunch; tap, tap, tap of the walking pole. Overhead, a few wispy clouds passed calmly and hypnotically and by looking up at them with gratitude it was possible to be tugged along further until there was a feeling of riding the light, riding the heat.

Shaking my head, we walked slowly to the vantage point we'd aimed for and it was immediately clear that the suffering had been worth it: the view of Noravank, a masterwork of architecture, made my heart throb with joy. A religious showpiece of the Caucasus, protected by its location, its built form melding effortlessly with its natural setting, offering a visual harmony, the ancient building not at all out of place among rocks, ridges and mountains. A holy tableau. We drank in the view until, unable to take the savage sun any more, we headed back down the stony way to see the complex up close.

As we scuttled downwards, my mind cast about. I thought of Rose Macaulay, bestselling novelist and untiring journeywoman who loved the sea and adventure, but to my disappointment was not much of a walker. In her whimsical book *Personal Pleasures*, she explained that for her walking encouraged a vacancy of mind and that it was a tedious and placid activity.

Joining the crowds and dusting ourselves off, I concluded that maybe if Macaulay had come here she might have changed her mind. After all, what can be sweeter than slogging up a hot hill to be met with a godly view and afterwards to be rewarded again by stepping into a thick-walled, and vastly cooler, church?

Scattered around Noravank are remnants of chapels and tombs, some dating back to the 5th century. Worn down over time, what secrets they must hold of long winters and stifling summers, of the years before cars made the journey here a possibility for those merely curious, not just the few seeking a monastic life. Even the sky above Noravank seemed old and I imagined what it must be like at night with the stars unimpeded by light pollution, glittering.

Inside, I felt a little envy at visitors who, bolstered by their faith, ancient culture and the spirit of Armenia, perceived and sensed so much more than me as they gazed up towards the carving of Christ above the door. Everyone was busy acting out the best versions of themselves, speaking quietly, standing upright, then carefully walking out again backwards, so as not to turn their back on the holiness within, before gathering again in groups to be photographed. Outside, perilous-looking cantilevered steps lead up narrowly on the facade to the upper storey. Things you cannot see clearly, nor feel as deeply, from the trailheads above.

How does Noravank look close up? To cut many corners, the largest two-storey building is the church of the Holy Mother, where the burial vault is the first floor, and above it is the oratory. The 13th-century architect Momik whose life is shrouded with many legends, is central to Noravank's story. One tale claims that Momik was in love with a beautiful daughter of an Orbelian prince. In exchange for her hand, the prince asked Momik to build him a chapel unlike any other. Momik nearly completed his work but didn't finish the dome, because he was pushed off the building by the orders of the prince and plunged to his death. It is also possible that in the 14th century learned monks began work on one of the great Armenian manuscripts here, the *Gladzor Gospels* (1300–07). The building was badly damaged in the 1840 earthquake and the lost cupola was not restored until the late 1990s. Only by standing alongside Noravank can you see the front wall has an eagle carrying a gazelle, the emblem of the Orbelian dynasty.

## TO THE CANYON TAVERN

While we had to use the car to drive into the dazzling valley, each line of hot hills nudging against another, approaching the ancient monastery by foot felt entirely right. Walking is so simple, so natural, that there is something holy about not just pilgrimages but the basic everyday practice of it. Anglican priest Adam Ford wrote in his recent book *The Art of Mindful Walking* '… it is interesting to remember that the disciples were on a walk with Jesus, away from the crowds, when they had their transfiguration experience.'

Later, in Yerevan, my Armenian friend, Luba Balyan, would introduce me to one of the longstanding priests of Noravank, a gregarious man by the name of Sahak Martirosyan. But now it was time to eat and to find the cave café. We walked along a track for a mile or so in full sun, until, to our relief, the Qarandzav Tavern announced itself almost too easily, with a road sign.

Indoors, the grotto was decorated with rugs and dried posies collected from around the valley – flowers I could not even bluff at knowing – and we were soon guided to a shady table outside where the warm air smelled of beer, fried meat and fire-baked lavash. The lunch was heartening: tomato and dill salad, cold and slightly sour thick madzoon (similar to yogurt), and best of all, a light but filling dish of fresh eggs lightly scrambled with purslane. Big glass bottles of ice-cold Jermuk mineral water. All of it so wonderfully effective at stripping away fatigue.

# Scrambled Eggs with Purslane and Paprika

This is a recipe based on the tavern lunch we ate near Noravank Monastery. Herby and tangy, purslane is an ancient salad ingredient that is frustratingly hard to find in the UK though it is commonly used by cooks in countries such as Lebanon, Egypt, Armenia and Turkey. For this recipe you can substitute it with rocket (arugula) or baby spinach (add ½ teaspoon of lemony-tasting sumac if using the latter to pep it up). Great for breakfast, this dish also proves that greens, not just herbs, can go very well with eggs.

**SERVES 1**

2 large eggs

Sea salt flakes and freshly ground black pepper

1 tbsp olive oil

½ red onion, finely chopped

½ green bell pepper, seeds removed, finely chopped

45g/1½oz purslane, shredded, or substitute as above

¼ tsp paprika

Sumac (optional)

In a bowl, beat together the eggs with salt and pepper and set aside. Heat a non-stick frying pan over a medium heat, add ½ tablespoon of the oil and cook the onion and green pepper until slightly softened (about 5 minutes). Add the purslane (or substitute) and sprinkle over the paprika, adding a pinch of salt, and stir, just for a minute or so, until the greens have wilted. Drizzle over the remaining ½ tablespoon of oil, then slowly pour in the egg mixture, let it rest in the heat for 5 seconds, then stir gently – you want it to scramble slowly and for everything to retain some shape. Dust with sumac, if using, season with salt and pepper and serve with flatbread or toast.

# DIVING INTO THE AQUATIC ALCHEMY OF JERMUK

At every hour, from sunrise to sunset, Jermuk's famous mineral water gallery, cool, colonnaded and built in the 1950s, is lined with people. They stand and queue and chat, waiting their turn, shoulder to shoulder, many clutching a prescription instructing them on how much to drink from which fountain, and at what temperature. On reaching the front of the line, a mug, cup or flask is raised to wall-mounted spigots from which water, heated somewhere between 30°C and 53°C, pours continuously into the neoclassical urns below. Occasionally, a child is lifted, open-mouthed, to drink directly from the tap.

Since we'd touched down in Armenia we'd drunk gallons of fizzy and restorative Jermuk and so I wanted to see for myself the high mountain resort town from where the bottled water took its name, surrounded by green forested hills and cascading waterfalls, such as Mermaid's Hair Falls. All so cooling on the eyes. And all so entirely different from the hot, dry Vayots Dzor region we'd known so far.

Joining the crowd we stood out as we'd arrived not for cure but out of curiosity and, unlike others queuing, we were without papers from a doctor. What we did have in common with everyone else was that we were also staying at one of the town's various sanatoriums and Soviet-era 'rest houses' which took the place of standard hotels and offered the greatest number of beds at the lowest prices. The Constitution Day holiday meant that many rooms were booked out and we'd had to plump for one of the more run-down options. The bed sagged and the staff were either absent, asleep in the corners of their elbows, or grumpy. We chose badly and were badly served as a result. Still, the location was central and the cool air outside was soothing.

To reach Jermuk, from the bone-dry canyons around Noravank, we had taken a detour, led away from the Jermuk highway to the 10th-century monastery of Gndevank, its little signpost on the road encouraging us towards it.

### APRICOTS FOR JAM, AND SIBERIA

Leaving the highway behind, the Lada bumped along an appallingly potholed road that had been repeatedly knocked about by earth tremors and landslides. Nonetheless, it led us up most of the way, past the canyon's huge cliff walls, peculiarly ribbed in long straight lines, giving the appearance of giant pipe organs shooting up from the ground. To save the tyres, and our spines, we got out to walk to Gndevank, the Lada having managed most of the 15 or so kilometres.

Light fell in shards through the tree branches, dazzling and dancing onto our hot shoulders as we followed the shaded path up to the church which, renovated in the 1960s following an earthquake, was dedicated to St Stepanos, as a nearby sign explained. Soon, the classical conical cupola came into view and as we approached it, not a sound could be heard other than our own footsteps and the buzzing of insects.

Galoshes and sandals were strewn outside the monk's cells, protected by an ancient dry-stone wall in which two small khachkars, cross-stones, had been artistically set about a couple of metres up. Beehives, painted baby blue and shaded by vines, lined the track to the church's open door. Small wooden ladders lay about, discarded in the tall grass, presumably for climbing up the fruit trees. Inside, I picked out a lace scarf from the jumble of head coverings by the door and moved towards the altar where candles had burned down to nubs, crossing over rugs in autumn hues of red and orange. Above, a giant chandelier glittered. The interior of the church had the same familiar feeling found in all places of worship, a sense of frozen time and of stepping into a shared human past: a connected community space of exaltation, dignity and beauty, of sadness and grief, of festivities and everydayness where silence is felt not as an oppressive force but as a welcome to focus the mind and human heart. Churches in Armenia, to be present in, to stand in awe of, are loved unconditionally for they contain so much of the beauty and pain that is felt in the world.

We nosed about, admiring the paintings of evangelists and saints, while the headscarf I had tied under my chin scented my hair with the smell of incense. Then, stooping to exit, we followed ancient carved stones, one showing two ibex butting heads, another a hunter mounted on horseback, around the boundary of the church where a signpost with a picture of a snake on it warned of what could be hiding in the long scrub. Cautiously, we walked back to the car and carried on back down the road but we were soon distracted again. Something through the bug-spattered window moved in the distance.

At the bottom of the valley, a large group of people were engaged in what looked like a giant picnic under some shade-giving trees. As we stopped the car and got out, we realised that they were not resting in the heat of the day but working on a project.

'Watch out for snakes,' said James needlessly as we walked down a steep slope towards them, a wobbly line of hills and the church in the far distance. A classical landscape. The heat, combined with the sharp descent, sent my heartbeat pulsing in my ears again. It soon became clear that the group were not sitting on an orange rug, as had first appeared, but were surrounded by thousands of apricots.

They spotted us and waved, calling us to come over. As we got closer, the air became weighed down with a sweet, fruity, sugary scent.

A man who seemed to be in charge, dressed in an Airtex T-shirt and chinos, introduced himself as Garik. Chewing on sunflower seeds, a snack ubiquitous in the Caucasus, he pointed up the valley and began to tell us, in Russian (still spoken widely in Armenia), what they were up to.

'We have a team of fifteen up the mountain picking apricots and eight of us here are sorting them. It'll take us three days in all to fill the lorry over there. Every year we buy the rights to pick from trees here and then what we can collect goes into the truck. The best apricots will go to Russia, the others will be sent to a local factory for jam.'

All around lay the juiciest-looking fruit. The group of workers knew what to look out for as they were, Garik told us, from Ararat province, a part of Armenia famous for its world-class apricots. The truck, a huge Volvo lorry imported from the Netherlands, its front windscreen kept cool by a blue lacy curtain, would travel slowly for five days or so to a food market in Omsk, Siberia. We wanted to know who in the group would drive the truck such a long way. 'Me!' Garik chuckled, jangling the ignition key in his hand. Life looked easy here, but of course it wasn't.

'Before, I was working on the road maintenance in Siberia. This is my first year doing this,' he added, taking a bite of an apricot and handing me a bag that weighed at least two kilos, 'A gift, take it.' I protested at such generosity of these fruity treasures, the pride of Armenia, but of course to no avail. 'Take it, take it. Please.'

'Why Omsk, not Moscow?' we asked.

'Nobody was delivering fruit of this quality there. I saw an opportunity. Of course they have other apricots in Omsk, but not like these. These we call Armenian Dawn apricots.'

I bit into one, the fleshy orange pulp firm (not at all cottony, as is sometimes the way with lesser apricots), tasting of apricot of course but also quince and apple and young grass somehow. A delight, a wonder, the fruit eaten close to where it grew. So good that you could never have enough. A feeling, a taste, impossible to recapture. Still, I tried there and then to mentally bank the flavours.

'We cannot get apricots like this in Britain,' we lamented to which we were rightly told, 'Because you don't have Armenian apricots in your country.'

'Vodka?' Garik asked with an uptick in his voice and a thrust of the chin. 'No, thank you,' we replied, explaining that we had to drive to Jermuk.

We shook hands and as I turned to wave goodbye I saw Garik was watching us as we walked away. Having put the apricots in the boot of the Lada, we drove on following the Arpa River into ever higher hills all the while the air becoming cooler, the scenery greener and lusher.

## GOOD CLIMATE, GOOD WATER

At 2,000 metres above sea level, Jermuk, its name derived from the Armenian for warm mineral spring, was wet and glinting, misty and mellow. After a sleepless night at the sanatorium, on an impossibly lumpy mattress, I left behind its clinical halls of medical consulting rooms (prices to stay were inclusive of treatments regardless of whether you took them or not), stopping first at a giant mural close to the main building, which thankfully had been preserved while construction, with cranes and bulldozers, banged on around it.

The mosaic depicted a boy in a Greek-style loincloth, holding his hands up to the sun, his wan face framed by hair spread out as sunrays, and with fruit trees surrounding him. Rivers lapped about his calves. El Masudi, the Arab traveller, born in Baghdad in the 9th century and known as 'Herodotus of the Arabs', wrote of Caucasians that 'they dress in white, in Greek brocade'. Greeks have lived in Armenia since ancient times, with many more moving to work in the rich copper mines to the north of the country in the 18th century.

Buoyed by the sinus-clearing, pine-scented breeze, I walked through the town pulling nourishing cool air into my lungs, gentle sounds falling on all sides: birdsong and the chatter of breakfasting Armenian tourists who'd arrived to drink the famous revitalising water at source, eager to hand themselves over to their chosen sanatorium, to drink the water of their ancestors and to do so in air neither dusty nor polluted. To feel the water of the rivers and waterfalls, to sense the healthful immersion of hot and cold baths. Each experience intensifying the other.

Drinking the water of Jermuk and again figuring out why it tastes better, cleaner, more cleansing, more refreshing, than other water; smell, sight and memory just as important as flavour. There was a purity to it all and the act of making a pilgrimage to the spa town seemed to be an almost religious experience.

The thermal water, rich with the sort of microchemical elements that if you aren't scientific do not sound appealing, is said to be in line with other notable spa resorts elsewhere – Karlovy Vary in the Czech Republic (where Tsar Peter the Great stayed for treatments) and Zheleznovodsk in Russia (where there is a 350-kilo bronze statue commemorating enemas).

In Armenia and Georgia you sometimes hear people saying 'good climate, good water' when they explain the appeal of a place. Memories of, and feelings around, water are not just to do with drinking it but the impact it has on the terrain, how its quality affects the health of trees, which then influences the quality of their nuts and fruit, just as the water you use to cook with, to soak your rice in, to add to your bread dough, alters flavours and outcomes.

But there are other reasons why Armenians come here, in the footsteps of their forefathers, that are far harder to quantify.

Water is fixed and fastened to national pride. Names, designs and colours of bottled water evoke a country: think of Italian Acqua Panna, Evian from the French Alps or Voss from Norway. It isn't simply a drink. It speaks of place, location and history, and it promises purity, cleanliness, even saintliness.

The green bottles of Jermuk, instantly recognisable with their metallic blue labelling, are positioned as a symbol for the entire country, appealing to national identity and nostalgia, which when combined, are exceptionally powerful. It isn't 'just' water, it is filled with associative sensory memories, revered and sacred. Distinctive and marketable since its beginnings as bottled water in the 1950s, everyone drinks it just as everyone knows the legend on the label, the logo of the deer: how, many years ago, a hunter wounded a deer with an arrow but the animal got away and limped to Jermuk. Completely exhausted, it jumped into the mineral-rich water and, as if by miracle, emerged fully healed.

Water in mountainous Armenia is generally dependable and there are splashing public drinking fountains, called pulpulaks (a word meaning drinking fountain that fizzes on the tongue), available in most towns, but bottled water sells here for exactly the same reasons it sells everywhere else: because of the social construction of purity, which is promoted through advertising. Despite the environmental impact, and anti bottled-water activism, bottled water has become a cultural norm.

How does Jermuk taste? Drunk from glass bottles (which makes all sparkling water taste better, crisper, fresher than water drunk from plastic), it is a little nose-tickling, marginally saline and very slightly bitter from the carbonic acid. Like any good seltzer, it can ease indigestion and clear the throat, just as it can shake up the brain a bit, while invigorating the palate. The bubbles are tiny and the minerality high.

Continuing my urban amble, I went on past the Moscow Sanatorium – one of the grander options in town – where in a field to the side, was an everyday yet eye-catching sight: dozens of pillowcases, of the purest white, immaculately pegged and spaced on their laundry line, moving orchestrally in the breeze. I sipped from my bottle of Jermuk and filmed it. The whiteness, the idea of cleaning, washing with water, new starts, freshness. It seemed a metaphor for the whole town.

That night, James and I returned to the water gallery with three Armenians from our hotel, walking there together, past the stands of pine trees and cafés that all played the songs of Charles Aznavour who, born in Paris in 1924, became known as the 'Frank Sinatra of France' but was the son of Armenians who'd fled the massacres in Turkey. Living in Tyumen in Siberia, the trio were on a ten-day family holiday as grandmother, mother and daughter, three generations and almost identical in looks, except for age. As we waited, paper cups in hand, we laughed as they joked about how they'd gotten rid of the men for their break and were enjoying the summer fruits, water and being together.

They agreed with us that the sanatorium food at our creaking hotel was not up to much and not 'real Armenian food' (which tends to be exceptional). The food was, in truth, dismal. Breakfast was highly processed cheese, kasha (buckwheat groats), shocking-pink frankfurters and roundels of other super-processed meat. Old-fashioned Soviet-style factory fare. During the Soviet era, 30,000 tourists a year would visit the town; now less than a quarter of that number show up. People simply no longer seek out sanatoriums like they used to, preferring instead yoga pavilions and luxury spas. Even so, the sanatoriums carry on, priding themselves on curing everything from digestive tract disorders to diabetes.

The general rule, the Armenian family explained to us, was that the water ought to be drunk 30 minutes before eating three times a day, and just an inch or so as it has a high salinity. Early evening was, therefore, rush hour at the fountains as everyone turned up to sip their water, at the prescribed temperature, before returning for their all-inclusive sanatorium dinner.

As a firm convert to Jermuk water, believing that an ice-cold glass of it was capable of improving most situations, especially hangovers, I was surprised, during my research, to learn that not so long ago, a scandal had unfolded.

In 2007, US health authorities banned sales of Jermuk claiming that it contained excessive amounts of arsenic. The Food and Drug Administration (FDA) ordered all importers of Jermuk to recall the product which was mainly sold in California where large numbers of Armenians live. On testing the water, the FDA claimed to have found between 500 and 600 micrograms of arsenic (which occurs naturally in the Earth's crust) per litre. 'FDA's standard of quality bottled water allows no more than 10 micrograms per litre', the agency was reported as saying.

While the FDA argued that extended exposure to the poisonous metal could in theory lead to cancer, it also added that so far there have been no recorded cases of illnesses caused by Jermuk. To add to the confusion, the Armenian National Institute of Standards was quick to state that it allows for up to 700 micrograms of arsenic in a litre of mineral water. The recall swiftly prompted coverage in the Armenian press, with government officials defending the water. Sales in Los Angeles, home to many Armenians, rocketed in defiance. There was never any danger of Armenians turning their back on their beloved Jermuk. As I write, a quick online search of American grocery stores shows Jermuk is freely, and widely, available again.

Before we left, we returned one last time to the drinking gallery at sunset. The water, warm but not hot from the particular tap we drank from, was slightly briny and a little tongue-prickling but most of all it was thought-provoking. When you drink the ancient waters of Jermuk, and you drink it mindfully, you share some of the same emotions as Armenians who have drunk it before you, even those early explorers who came here, drew the waters and immediately knew the value of what they had found.

The next day, we'd leave for the capital, Yerevan. Nature in Vayots Dzor, the canyons, hills, flowers and the spa town of Jermuk had restored and generously replenished in us what big city living is so good at stripping away, that is energy, sanity, and general wellbeing. But balance is needed, you need both. There is no denying the joy of what it is to temporarily become part of a city's fabric, its daily life and common appetites. And the best way to do that is to walk it.

# Armenian Dawn

This cocktail, named after the Armenian Dawn variety of apricots being sorted by Garik and his team (see page 51), is fragrant and summery and, with the modest addition of brandy and almond, a little punchier than the traditional Bellini it resembles. Great for a garden party.

**MAKES 1 COCKTAIL**

2 apricots, pitted

Small dash of almond extract

1 tbsp brandy

170ml/generous ⅔ cup prosecco, chilled

Pulse the apricots in a food processor until you have a purée and stir through the almond extract. Spoon 1–2 tablespoons of purée into a glass and add the brandy. Top up with the prosecco, and stir.

# Lamb with Plums, Green Beans and Cinnamon

This fine spirited meal-in-one showcases fruit in a savoury dish – ideal for late spring or summer when nature's gates are thrown open, providing an abundance of garden herbs, fresh vegetables and fruit.

**SERVES 2 GENEROUSLY**

2 tbsp olive oil

500g/1lb 2oz lamb shoulder, chopped into small bite-size pieces

Sea salt and freshly ground black pepper

1 onion, thinly sliced

2 garlic cloves, thinly sliced

130g/4½oz green beans, chopped into 4cm/1½in pieces

1 tsp ground cinnamon

½ tsp sweet paprika

1 tbsp tomato purée (paste)

1 tbsp red wine vinegar

4 plums, stoned and chopped into bite-size pieces

500ml/2 cups vegetable stock

2 tbsp flat-leaf parsley, finely chopped

Juice of ½ lemon

In a casserole dish with a lid, heat 1 tablespoon of the oil. Season the meat and fry briefly until browned. Remove from the pan with a slotted spoon and add the remaining oil. Add the onion, garlic and beans, and fry with a little salt and pepper – if it is catching add a little more oil – and stir continuously. Cook for 5 minutes until soft, then add the spices, tomato purée, vinegar and plums, cook for another 5 minutes, then add the stock. Return the lamb to the pan. Simmer gently, uncovered, for 15 minutes (you want to thicken it), then for 10 more minutes with the lid on. Let it sit for a while to let the flavour develop, then scatter over the parsley, stir through the lemon juice and serve in bowls with crusty white bread on the side.

# ROVING THROUGH YEREVAN
# AND THE HISTORY OF THE NEW

Luba Balyan, scientist, esteemed birdwatcher and dear friend of mine, leaned on the table of a café in downtown Yerevan, and wiped the sweat from her forehead.

'The key is not to go fast, Caroline, don't wear yourself out. Later, I'll meet you by the Chess House. Then you can carry on with your walk and I'll see you for dinner with the priest, such a wonderful individual he is. There is a lot to see, it is true, but also it is so hot. Be careful!'

The city's heatwave had gotten worse by the day, with temperatures above 30°C before breakfast. I'd accepted that any ambition to walk the city, to peel back its layers, meant doing so languidly. While I knew it would be pointless trying to be too determined, I also didn't want to waste energy. I'd stroll with slow purpose, more pedestrian than flâneuse (too aimless), stopping as needed.

As I set off, thoughts crowded my mind: *Will the city live up to what I'd imagined it to be? What of the atmosphere? Would it feel nationalistic? What would the language of the buildings be like? Would the streets smell of cognac and cigars as I imagined they might? What of the café rituals? And where would the very heart of Yerevan be found or, at least, felt?*

I began with brunch on the outskirts of the city centre at a no-nonsense roadside place called Merhatsy. This meant: a plate of fattoush, a basket of puff lavash plus a bowl of super-soft hummus, dusted with za'atar and paprika, and with a compression in the centre holding a few small ribbons of chopped parsley and three buttery whole chickpeas swimming in a pool of greenish olive oil.

Postcards inside the café, of Beirut's corniche, hinted at the homeland of the owners. Yerevan has seen a newish-wave of restaurants opened by ethnic-Armenians from Lebanon and Syria who have returned (or been 'repatriated', as locals say), escaping war and economic collapse in those countries. Collectively, they have changed the dining scene in Yerevan. They speak Arabic, Armenian and English and serve, usually with lashings of charm and chat, mint tea with tabbouleh, labneh and what are surely some of the best salads in the world. At Zeituna, an insanely popular and busy restaurant in the very centre of town, open since 2012 when the family arrived from Syria, the cooks make freekeh with lamb topped with toasted cashews and almonds, and samsak urfa, little savoury tarts filled with mince. During my time in Yerevan, most days I ate one meal in either a Syrian- or Lebanese-run café. It is exactly the sort of food you want to eat in heat that knocks you out.

At Merhatsy, I drank the dregs of my ice-cold Jermuk and scooped up the last of the hummus and felt grateful to be there, sitting at a Coca-Cola branded table, watching people coming and going from the gigantic cathedral across Yervand Kochar Street, which is named after the sculptor. In Yerevan, you read a street name and inevitably it leads to a writer or artist, a poet or a mystic bard, then you need to know when they lived, what they did, who they married, when they died and of what. Like in most big cities, a rabbit warren of discoveries, and possibilities, present themselves at every step.

Gathering myself, I paid then crossed the road to a supermarket. In front of the chiller, I stopped under a blast of air conditioning and scanned the Ararat-branded bottles of kompot on offer: blackcurrant, pear, cornelian cherry, yellow cherry, strawberry and feijoa. I settled on raspberry then stepped out into the sauna-like heat, wiping the fridge-cold condensation from the bottle onto my hot wrists.

## BISHOPS, KINGS AND TIGRAN PETROSIAN

Crossing the road to the cathedral opposite, I craned my neck to see its grandiose rectangular belfry and the cross that marks the very top, at 54 metres. Named for the patron saint who converted Armenia to Christianity in the 4th century, Gregory the Illuminator is monumental with two chapels and a grand nave but stepping inside it felt unsatisfying somehow. A vast space with a weirdly unresponsive air. Lacking in tenderness.

My architectural guidebook entitled *Yerevan* which features the church in one of its many walking routes, offered a clue to the chilliness: 'in mediaeval times natural stone lay at the foundation of the entire structural system for a church; here it plays a decorative role as cladding for the reinforced concrete framework.' It reminded me of Tbilisi's Holy Trinity Cathedral, completed in 2004 and known as Sameba, with its enormous scale and icons dripping with glitter and gold and gems, Byzantine-looking and with the capacity for over 10,000, but with no scent of the ages, no rugs worn thin by countless congregations. Impressive but too shiny. Holy places need to be worn in, to gather spiritual gravitas by accumulating prayers, hopes and life events over decades. The very things that St Paul and Peter Church, once located on Yerevan's fashionable Abovyan Street and dating back all the way back to the 5th century, was surely enormously rich with, until it was mindlessly destroyed in the 1930s, during the Soviet period, to make room for the Moscow Cinema.

Keeping the cathedral to my left, I walked into Circular Park, past a statue of Taras Shevchenko, Ukraine's national poet, unveiled in 2018 to mark a hundred years of diplomatic relations between the two countries and a nod to the tens of thousands of ethnic Armenians living in Ukraine. Groups of men clustered under trees were drinking tea and pushing chess pieces back and forth. Armenia is a land of chess, producing a disproportionate number of grandmasters for its small size, and this sight served as a taster for my next stop.

My friend Luba was waiting for me in a slice of shade outside the modernist Chess House, completed in 1970 and named after Tigran Petrosian who won the world championship in 1963 and defended his title three years later. She explained that, along with many of the city's best buildings, it was built with tuff, compacted deposits of volcanic detritus. The exterior, striking enough that it features on a banknote, has eye-catching bas reliefs of chess pieces but that is nothing compared to the interior.

Inside, we first passed hushed tables of children playing chess (the game has been on the primary school curriculum since 2011), then, opening a heavy wooden door, we entered the main tournament room. Empty of players, it was alive with huge tapestries depicting bishops and kings, priests and decorated stallions. Below the framed textiles, wooden tables with chess boards on their tops stood on Armenian rugs. A portrait of Petrosian watched over the space from the back wood-panelled wall. Mesmerising and unexpected, it was simply one of the most fantastic rooms I'd ever seen.

Luba, who knows everyone, introduced me to the director, Hrachik Tavadyan. Sitting in his office, framed by shelves of trophies and a large Armenian flag, he was as solemn as he was quietly spoken. Timidly, I asked for his top tips.

'It's a physical sport, so don't sit for the full game. Move about. And remember patterns.'

In the Chess House garden we posed for a photograph by a statue of Petrosian. Then Luba's phone rang and she walked away to take the call. 'That was Father Sahak, we'll meet tonight at eight. Don't be late!' A quick kiss and she was off.

## TREASURED MEDIEVAL ELIXIRS

Chess connected my walk nicely to the next stop, Yerevan's star landmark, the Matenadaran (book depository). Among its collection of ancient Armenian manuscripts the library holds 12th-century documents mentioning the game.

But there were other things to see first. Continuing along the ring road, the guidebook led me to the Yeritasardakan metro station. Completed in 1981, it would be unremarkable if not for one thing: a gigantic tilted cylindrical tube jutting out widely from the subterranean station. Brutalist and futuristic, the purpose of the glass-fronted concrete chute is to funnel light into the gloom below.

Slayed by the heat, I drifted towards a splashing pulpulak. Bending down woozily, I gulped the cool water. Some of Yerevan's pulpulaks are artistically carved from stone and some serve as memorials to the dead, a bit like a bench with a plaque and a view. Free, useful and available to everyone. To drink in their memory, to be blessed and refreshed by it. And with the bowing down to drink, the lowering the head, a paying of respect.

But the pulpulak also struck me to the point of sadness. It made me think of how poorly served we are in the UK, and how it wasn't always so. In 19th-century Britain the need for clean water led to a new and magnificent genre of folly fountains, the grander ones with granite bowls and made of filigree and cast iron and decorated with crocketed spires. They have since dwindled because they fell apart through lack of care or were vandalised and taken away. And because simple things that serve the people, and that do not relate to money, are not valued. Armenians have many ways of glorifying water. There are goddesses – such as Tzovinar or Nar, goddess of water, sea and rain, and Astłik, goddess of fertility and water springs – there is the pagan water festival of Vardavar, dating back to ancient times, and mythical dragon stones called vishapakars dotted about the countryside, protectors and spirits of water.

The pulpulak I stopped at was on a street named after Byron, the English poet, because he had studied Armenian at the Armenian monastery on the Venetian island of San Lazzaro during the winter of 1816, and this has been fondly remembered.

I walked on, going up Mashtots Avenue, named after Mesrop Mashtots, believed by many to be the creator of the Armenian alphabet in the 5th century, until I reached the austere Matenadaran. Symmetrical and standing alone, it appeared like a temple or a fortress.

Inside the grey basalt building, constructed in stages between 1945 and 1959, there are gospels held in ivory bindings a thousand years old. Armenian bibles printed in Amsterdam in 1666. Glass cabinets of medieval elixirs, consecrated oils, and the royal elixir, made according to encrypted medical recipes and special distillation technology, used by kings to maintain youthfulness. Preserved in oak barrels, and suitable to keep for years, there is much ceremony attached to collecting and harvesting of the rare mountainous herbs that go into the royal elixir. Rules laid out in the manuscripts suggest foraging on certain days which improves the potion's strength, and ingredients include extracts from 54 aromatic herbs, roots and flowers, including mountain honey, nutmeg, dried iris bulbs and Armenian hawthorn. Medieval physicians believed that the elixir 'heals the heart and makes the spirit happy'.

Also on display is the *Homilies of Mush*, a mammoth 13th-century manuscript, weighing 28 kilos and made of hundreds of calfskins. It was split in two by a pair of women who saved it from a monastery in Mush (now Muş, in present-day Turkey) while fleeing the genocide of 1915.

Such insurmountable circumstances are etched into Armenia's shared consciousness and collective memory: the earthquake of 1988, which destroyed buildings and killed tens of thousands in the northwest; the socio-economic hardships of independence in 1991, when pianos were burned as firewood to keep homes warm; and most recently the loss of Nagorno-Karabakh. It all pains the heart.

### SALT LADIES AND THE GODDESS ANAHIT

For all that, in Yerevan hope and humour can always be found, and a sense of spectacle. There is the constant chatter from pavement cafés and the sound of Charles Aznavour's honeyed voice spilling out from speakers, men belly-laughing and billowing cigar smoke, the tantalising smell of barbecuing meat known as khorovats and best of all, on street corners, fruit ripening in cardboard boxes, buckets and washing-up bowls. Sweet apricots in particular, their skin velvety soft, their intense scent cracked open by the burning sun.

But perhaps nowhere displays parade and performance better in Yerevan than the Vernissage open market where I wandered to next, with one eye on lunch, heading straight for its shady awnings.

In the thin lanes are things you find at markets across the Caucasus (and Ukraine and Central Asia), things that exude nostalgia. Dusty old atlases of the USSR, golden icons, ceramics decorated with pomegranates, table runners stitched with grapes and vines. And stacks upon stacks of old vinyl. The usual Elvis and Boney M, but also recordings of Armenian folk singers, including Djivan Gasparyan, master of the duduk, the instrument carved out of apricot wood.

One welcomingly sunless stall I lingered at was selling something new to me: suitcases containing all that is needed for making shashlik. Pop the clasps, flip open the shiny faux crocodile-skin case – et voilà! – a set of steel plates, skewers, shot glasses, playing cards, carving knives, a corkscrew, hip flask and even a small axe. But I'd not come for that. What I wanted was a salt lady. If you stay in Armenia long enough you start to notice unusual-looking salt cellars, human-shaped figurines, some with arms as handles. In Armenia, salt is always on the table not just for taste and to excite the appetite but because it is 'a divine substance', as Homer once said of it. Historically, Armenians would spill salt to form a white cross on the ground during bad storms, inhospitable people might have been referred to as 'people without bread and salt', whereas those who shared bread and salt together would likely become allies.

Salt cellars are always female in form, ceramic figurines that are often brightly painted, or else left as unglazed terracotta. More often than not, their faces are expressional: little mouths in an 'o', eyes wide, eyebrows raised, a look of surprise, saying 'Look at me!' Some of the earliest examples of salt ladies show a face on the neck of the jar, with the hole to reach the salt via the mouth, while the rarest ones are depicted with children held on the hip, or under arms. Others have a baby in the womb depicted on their bellies. Some antique salt ladies are more abstract, impressed with marks and decorated, though perhaps not with facial features, while others appear like female centaurs. Most have an opening to access the salt via the navel, suggesting fertility. In ancient Armenia, new mothers and midwives would wash themselves with salt, in a custom called the first christening (both a purification and protection practice), and the baby would have a little salt rubbed on their stomach, too.

Potters today make smaller salt jars, about 20 centimetres tall – half the size of the 19th-century version – for use in modern kitchens, and even smaller ones to stand on the table as a decoration. Salt lady amulets can also be bought to wear around the neck on a chain.

Finally, at one stall selling terracotta plates and jugs I spotted a crowd of salt ladies. I asked the seller about the price and what she thought about their origins.

'Salt was a gift from the goddess Anahit. So by keeping the salt within the womb of the goddess, the salt is blessed while the terracotta absorbs any moisture, so the salt stays dry in humid kitchens.' I thanked her as she bubble-wrapped my own salt lady to take home. The one I had chosen has the same surprised expression as the earlier ones I'd seen in old photographs and the top of her head has a hollow where you could, in theory, place a candle. Later, I read that when worship of the pagan goddess Anahit became controversial, as Armenia formally adopted Christianity, wooden salt birds were used instead as a way of getting round this as they too were symbols of Anahit, but in disguise.

It was time to stop for lunch. Tucked just behind the market is the palatial Tufenkian Hotel, built of orange and black tuff, and it is a reliable place. Sitting down, in the relief of air-conditioning, I ordered a large bottle of Jermuk, a citrus and walnut salad and a plate of eetch, a cooling Armenian dish that I had become quite obsessed with. It couldn't be simpler: fine bulgur infused with concentrated tomato juice topped with a salad of spring onions and red pepper (see my recipe on page 122). It was cool and soothing and, once it was over, I was prepared to return to the almost sizzling pavement outside.

Immediately, I stepped into a cloud of heady blue smoke coming from a nearby macho-luxe café where men sat al fresco on plush velveteen chairs, smoking cigars. I glanced towards the group and saw from their faces that they were in seventh heaven. Armenians have a long relationship with cigars. I thought of Avo Uvezian, an Armenian-American who was known for three things: his white suits, his talent as a jazz pianist and for being the man who sold the distribution rights of Avo cigars to Davidoff. Then, in London, there is Edward Sahakian, a man also impeccably dressed, who can often be spotted outside his Davidoff shop on the corner of Jermyn Street.

A few more minutes and I was on Republic Square, the city's traffic-choked core. There, I headed into the grand central post office, colonnaded, striking and built of pink tuff, material of the city's finest architecture. Inside, soaring above the main counter, is a giant stained-glass panel of doves, aeroplanes and trains delivering envelopes around the world, with Mount Ararat at the centre. 'I see Mount Ararat … with its gentle, tender contours it seems to grow not out of the earth but out of the sky', as the Russian writer Vasily Grossman had described it. To one side of the building stood a little shop selling presentation packs of postage stamps.

Aren't stamps the very best souvenirs? Small, generally affordable and portable. Sometimes pretty, sometimes weird, someday collectible. Flicking through folder after folder, each one showing Armenia in miniature, a small-scale travel brochure highlighting different seasons, animals, costumes, flora and wineries. I settled on a design by David Dovlatyan, a 300 dram stamp designed for 2021, featuring a single pumpkin, round, childlike, jolly, flumping and bodily in its curves. The pumpkin pictured on the stamp had been transformed, by the hands of a cook, into ghapama, filled with rice, dried fruit, nuts and honey, popular in the autumn and at Christmas. I bought two presentation packs. The shop was surprisingly busy. I asked the woman behind the counter whether this was typical.

'Yes, why? Everyone loves stamps and Armenians have a long history of winning designs. You chose well, I see,' she said matter-of-factly, looking at my pumpkin stamps before bagging them up.

## A SILVER WALNUT MOON

Republic Square is the very heart of the city, shaped by Russia-born Armenian architect Alexander Tamanian who relocated to Yerevan to help rebuild the city after it was named capital of the First Republic of Armenia in 1918. His masterplan for the city contained two of central Yerevan's masterpieces: the government house and the opera house, a short walk away. Tamanian wanted his architectural designs to symbolise the revival of Armenians and Armenia following the genocide of 1915. Intrinsic to his plan was a desire for Mount Ararat to be a central feature of the city, and, where possible, for buildings to be orientated towards it. But Tamanian could not have imagined the growth in residential mikrorayons (micro-districts) with their prefabricated panels and industrial zones which attracted villagers to work, boosting the population, and blocking views of Ararat.

Of Mount Ararat, James Morier, travel writer of the 19th century and assistant to the British ambassador in Turkey, had this to say: 'It is perfect in all its parts, no hard rugged feature, no unnatural prominences, everything is in harmony, and all combines to render it one of the sublimest objects in nature' although perhaps another British traveller put it better. H.F.B. Lynch, who visited Armenia twice – in 1893 and 1898 – and produced a two-volume book on the country. Having climbed Ararat he described it as having 'subtle grace' and standing 'like some vast cathedral, on the floor of the open plain'.

Walking on, I reached In Vino, one of those enticing bottle shops with an attached bar, and pavement seating, that makes it all too easy to linger. Red wines from the Ararat valley, such as those from Tushpa, are especially complex and moreish, and right opposite the bar is the handsome house museum of artist Martiros Saryan, striking with a mosaic of Mount Ararat on its facade. Two architectural greats were involved with the early designs, Tamanian and his successor as chief architect of Yerevan, Mark Grigorian, who also worked on the Matenadaran.

Saryan regularly entertained other artists and writers in his salon when he lived there: Sergei Parajanov, the great filmmaker of the Caucasus, John Updike, Benjamin Britten and the thrillingly non-conservative composer Aram Khachaturian, whose own house museum nearby is framed by five enormous white stone arches resembling tuning forks.

I'd spent the previous morning at the blissfully air-conditioned museum, meandering through Saryan's own Armenia, captured in oil and gouache, pastoral villages, courtyards, churches and paintings of Mount Ararat. But *Egyptian Masks*, painted in 1915, that terrible year for Armenians, was most memorable of all. Horror appears in the eyes of one mask, bewilderment in another, but there is stoicism and poise on the face of the golden mask. Scattered fruit lay all around the canvas, representing perhaps the Armenian diaspora. Saryan once described his work, and its ambition, as 'the visible survival of our small country after its tragic epic soaked in blood … I wish to show the world that this mountainous little country exists.' Words painfully relevant today and, like Yerevan's revealing architecture, that painting, and those words, will stay with me.

I wandered on. The entrances to courtyards, I noticed, were often stencilled with the same graffiti reading 'We Dance Together, We Fight Together' above a red death mask and a black helmet. Another popular one simply stated 'Defend Yerevan'. By now it was very late afternoon. A hot wind, blowing from the south-east, that started up reliably every day at the same time, was just easing off. People had begun to walk in that ceremonious style that comes with early evening in summer. But even towards sunset it was still unfathomably hot. Air-conditioning units dripped onto scalding pavements and outside cafés diners fashioned fans from something – anything – to hand, a napkin, a newspaper, a menu.

Finally, the Blue Mosque, my chosen boundary and finishing point for the walk.

Built in 1766, and reconstructed several times, it is surrounded by apartment blocks, but the front entrance, where boys kicked a football, is unmissable with its vaulted arch and blue ceramic tilework. During the Soviet era it was a natural history museum. I walked inside, going past a rose garden and an empty pool painted with the long shadows of the dome and walls. A Persian Cultural Centre had been installed but it was deserted. It all reminded me a little of Uzbekistan. There, too, you have tiled splendour standing in contrast with Soviet residential austerity. The elegance and freeflow of calligraphy and painted tulips on tiles jarring against the solid mass of modernist flats in the distance with their horizontal balconies as monotonous as graph paper. The past pushing against the past.

Afterwards, I went back to the apartment to lie down and cool off before meeting Luba and the priest. Swallows warbled in the sky, zipping through laundry lines strung between balconies ten floors up, pillowcases billowing like sails. By the time I woke up, night had fallen and a tiny silver walnut moon hung in the sky.

When walking through a city little known to you, it isn't the longitude or latitude that matters most but rather the attention paid, the feelings absorbed, and the possibilities of joy, of learning. Accepting that you might not find what you set out to discover, but something else instead.

# Ghapama – Rice-filled Pumpkin

Inspired by my purchase of Armenia's 300 dram stamp, designed by David Dovlatyan and featuring a single pumpkin, this is a fitting, and handsome, dish for autumn. Traditionally ghapama is made with honey but I prefer it without. You can always mix a teaspoon in with the chopped nuts and fruit if you fancy it sweeter.

**SERVES 4–6**

1 small pumpkin (roughly 1kg/2lb 4oz)

½ tbsp olive oil, plus extra for rubbing

1 tsp ground cinnamon

1 tsp dried chilli flakes

Sea salt and freshly ground black pepper

65g/2¼oz blanched whole almonds and hazelnuts

50g/1¾oz dried sour cherries and dried apricots

20g/¾oz raisins

80g/⅜ cup basmati rice, well rinsed

Juice of ½ lemon

Pinch of saffron strands, soaked in 1 tbsp warm water

15g/1 tbsp butter

Preheat the oven to 220°C/425°F/gas mark 7. Cut a lid off the pumpkin – take care here as this requires a sharp knife and surprisingly strong arms, and the skin is slippery – and reserve it. Scrape out the stringy bits and the seeds. Continue to cut a little more of the flesh until you have a shell that is roughly 2cm/¾in thick, keep any leftover flesh for soup. Rub the inside of the pumpkin, and the lid, with the oil, cinnamon, chilli, salt and pepper. Place on a baking tray and roast for 30 minutes.

Meanwhile, gently toast the nuts in a dry pan for 4–5 minutes until they start to pick up colour. Once cool, roughly chop them into small pieces along with the cherries and apricots. Put in a large bowl with the raisins and set aside.

Bring a pan of salted water to the boil. Boil the rice for 5 minutes before removing it from the heat, draining, and allowing to cool. Next, stir the cooled rice into the fruity nut mix, stir through the lemon juice and the saffron with its soaking water, and season well with salt and pepper. Heap into the pumpkin, top with the butter, and place the lid back on top.

Take roughly 70cm/28in of thick foil, then rub the pumpkin skin with a little oil, before wrapping with the foil. Place back on the tray and turn the oven down to 180°C/350°F/gas mark 4 and roast for a further 30 minutes to 1 hour, until the flesh is soft enough for a knife to pierce easily. Let it rest for 15 minutes, keeping the lid on to ensure that the rice is cooked properly, before serving, either hot or at room temperature. Definitely eat the pumpkin skin too (if soft enough) and either cut into wedges or invite people to scoop.

# Jingalov Hats – Herb-filled Flatbreads

On Yerevan's Komitas Avenue (named after Armenia's saintly singer) there is a traditional jingalov hats café and when the stuffed bread ('hats' means bread in Armenian) comes to you, warm and in the shape of a deflated rugby ball, it is often served with three bowls containing salt, cumin and paprika. Ingredients for the green filling vary, depending on what herbs are available, but typically this will include dill, coriander, greens (maybe spinach or sorrel) and spring onions.

I learned how to make jingalov hats at home using the book *Lavash* as my guide. Created by Kate Leahy, John Lee and Ara Zada it is an essential addition to your cookbook collection and a must for anyone interested in Armenia.

**MAKES 4**

**FOR THE DOUGH**

240g/1¾ cups plain (all-purpose) flour, plus extra for dusting

1 tsp fine salt

160ml/⅔ cup lukewarm water

**FOR THE FILLING**

500g/1lb 2oz greens – a combination of any of the following so you have ⅔ greens, ⅓ herbs: spring greens, Swiss chard (thick stems removed), spinach, rocket (arugula), coriander (cilantro), parsley, basil, dill, roughly chopped

6 spring onions (scallions), thinly sliced

1 tbsp vegetable oil, plus extra for frying

1 tsp salt

1 tsp black pepper

½ tsp sweet paprika

½ lemon, juiced

Put the flour in a large bowl and sprinkle in the salt. Make a well in the centre, pour in the lukewarm water and mix thoroughly. Turn onto a flour-dusted surface and knead for 10 minutes until the stickiness has gone (use a little more flour if needed) and the dough is soft. Form into a ball and put in a lightly oiled bowl, covered with a damp tea towel and let it rest for 30 minutes.

Wash all the greens, herbs and spring onions then heat a frying pan, add a little oil, and gently cook until everything has wilted. Put the lot into a colander to drain for a few minutes and, when cool, squeeze out as much of the liquid as possible, then mix with the oil, salt, black pepper, sweet paprika and lemon juice. Set aside.

Split the dough into 4 equal balls. Keep what you're not working with covered with a damp tea towel. Then, on a well-floured surface, roll one ball into a disc about 20cm/8in diameter – it should be lavash- (or tortilla-) thin. Spread a quarter of the greens over the dough, leaving a border of roughly 3cm/1¼in. You are now looking to create a flat rugby or American football shape so bring the two opposite sides of the disc together and pinch them firmly to seal until you have a large leaf-shaped flatbread. Turn it over and flatten gently with your hand, or a rolling pin, dispelling any air through gaps at either end before sealing those too. Repeat with the other balls.

When they're all done, heat a large frying pan over a medium heat, with a tiny amount of oil, and fry the hats, one at a time, turning regularly, pressing down to make contact every so often until lightly golden, flip and repeat until each one is cooked on both sides.

Serve warm.

# THE LIGHT IN WHICH WE WALK: DINNER WITH FATHER SAHAK MARTIROSYAN

Luba was already there, ushering me over to sit with her and Father Sahak Martirosyan, at a table under a giant mulberry tree in the centre of a courtyard restaurant on Abovyan Street in downtown Yerevan. After ordering a bottle of Jermuk, a jug of wild plum kompot and whizzing through introductions, Father Martirosyan, a man instantly likeable, began to speak of his life at Noravank Monastery, both as servant to God, and as witness to nature.

'Once, I was putting on my gown and I realised a scorpion was in there. I was bitten by yellow scorpions many times! When I was sleeping at 3a.m., it happened. It was very painful and I laid there wondering, "shall I go back to sleep or will I die?" But I knew the poison of these yellow ones was not so bad.' As he talked, mulberries, little oozing purple torpedoes, pinged off our shoulders from the tree above. Listening to him, I recalled the sweltering walk up high above the monastery, and imagined him there, in his black robes, in all seasons.

'Noravank is a fortress inside a fortress, the monastery created by man and the gorge, by nature. My neighbours there were mainly bezoar goats, I knew them all individually, and they knew me. And the donkeys and the white storks of Vayots Dzor.'

The bearded vultures, he explained, are perpetual patrollers, always ready to feast on the flesh of fallen goats. Then there are the bears who calmly lick ancient stones around the monastery, for salt. When the road was built to Noravank it was man not nature that won, he told us, but thanks to a regreening project, with new trees planted, nature is once again gaining ground.

'Noravank has become a resort for animals, a biodiversity hotspot. So much so that there are hundreds of snakes hanging from the trees in some parts of the valley. They are everywhere in summer. Armenian vipers, steppe vipers. Some are dangerous and very poisonous.'

Pouring out glass after glass of water and kompot, refreshing armour against the sticky night, Luba and I listened intently to Martirosyan's wildlife stories as he went on, his warm eyes lighting up with the tales. First ordained in 1997, and now retired from Noravank after 13 years there, he had a benevolence that flowed out of him, putting those in his company instantly at ease. He reached down and placed a plastic bag onto the table.

'This is my photography book of Noravank,' he began, laying it flat on the table for us to see. His passion for filming the monastery's surroundings started, he explained, when a Russian TV channel turned up. 'I simply followed them and saw what they photographed and thought I could do the same.' He modestly batted away the compliments Luba and I bestowed on him as we admired a picture of a cloud formation looking like Noah's ark.

Time rolled easily on. Luba was captivated, and in hysterics at Father's jokes half the time. They were old friends, catching up, while welcoming me into their fold.

## DIVINE JEST AND SORREL SALADS

But as the smell of khorovats wafted over us, I tried to ignore an increasingly gnawing appetite as one by one the photos continued to draw us away from the menu. I berated myself for casting the occasional jealous glimpse towards diners eating all around us.

'Once a hermit decided to travel from one monastery to another. On the way he is attacked by a bear. He runs but the bear bounds after him and the hermit ends up trapped by cliffs with nowhere left to run. He hears the bear growling, coming closer. He prays, "Oh my Lord can you please convert this bear to a Christian?" The bear stops, within a metre. The hermit thinks he is saved. But as he turns to move he stops in shock as the bear has miraculously begun praying. And what is it that the bear says? "Thank you God for granting this food to me!"' Luba howls and claps her hands. Father chuckles.

But the conclusion to the joke, Martirosyan tells us, has an important message. It is: you have to know what you are praying for. God simply awarded them both their wishes.

'I am not a good photographer, I just had plenty of time,' Martirosyan continued before telling us, with the smallest dash of pride, that he had once displayed his work at an exhibition in California.

Looking through the book it is clear he has ample talent. There is a bear cub peeking out from a cave ('I narrowly missed its mother'), a zoomed-in alien-looking praying mantis with an expressional face, and apricot trees in the snow. The road to holy Noravank often closes in winter. Electricity pylons come down.

'It often dropped as low as minus twenty but we had a big log-fired oven to keep warm. Over my gown I wore layers of coats and I didn't feel cold there because in cold weather you think clearly, and of good things. You have fire, a teapot. And, a guard who spoke very little, an important factor. Out there, there is a need for loud silence.' I nodded, my stomach now growling audibly.

Then we were into the details of his artistry, the geometry of light. He knows the position of the sun during every season, where and when the light will fall inside Noravank, the exact hour when strong rays shine upon the khachkars, making the stones glow golden and godly. On his mobile phone he showed us Pink Floyd album covers, and a clip of a satellite. Inspiration comes from different things and light is important to Father Martirosyan.

'When you come from a dark place into the light you have to orient yourself, take repose. In Armenia when someone dies, we say let the soul be enlightened, let it float in the light. People come in and out but the light always waits for them.'

Eventually, we placed a large order of suitably summery food. Cool tolma (rice and herbs wrapped in a grape leaf), bean pâté, grilled beef, salads of sorrel and tabbouleh, roast peppers and courgettes and a plate of fresh lavash.

Clinking our glasses of kompot when the colourful parade of dishes finally came to the table, I asked about the different ways to say 'cheers' in Armenian. They both think. 'One toast is simply "eh!" It is the shortest one, where you just drink,' Luba says. Sometimes, a toast will be the words 'stay alive', a plea more than a salute.

As Martirosyan eats the cubes of chargrilled beef, he pauses to talk about how different Armenia's cuisine today is compared to before.

'There are many things that were lost in western Armenia [eastern Turkey today]. The persecution was very prolonged, so we survived first and things were lost. Massacre, revolution, hunger, then a lot of expulsions. When a house was destroyed, things were lost. Livestock driven away. There was no time to think about cuisine. Then during communism there was scarcity in everything, there was little diversity. Collective farms killed competition and ingenuity. Culinary expression in that situation, in that society, was limited. For a long time the country looked more like a military camp.'

And now?

'I still don't see enough. The farmer just sells the meat, there is little imagination. And more waste now. We need to learn again about how to preserve and ways of traditional housekeeping. Today, rural dishes are very simple, not like in western Armenia before. I'd like to see farmers not just slaughtering to sell the meat but preserving it as well, to make basturma [pastrami-style beef] and other things.'

My mind wandered a little as we ate our bread, casting back to an ancient Armenian village belief that details how angels would fly around the tonir (clay oven) as lavash was being baked, cursing anyone who dared offend the bakers. The tonir has long been viewed as sacred. This particular lore was recorded by the scholar Yervand Lalayan who, in 1896, launched *Azgagrakan Handes* (*Ethnographic Journal*), which became a premier source for Armenian ethnology, folklore and archaeology. He also detailed how bread would never be thrown onto the ground (as is the case throughout Central Asia and elsewhere) as it had been blessed by the tonir, while the oven itself would be sanctified by the same water that had been used in the ritual washing of a child after their baptism.

Generally, there is a perception that priests ought to be serious, pious and detached, probably not interested in matters such as kitchen culture and photography, but Father Martirosyan, all quiet authority and easy smiles, is proof that isn't always so. He is modest, too, not just about his camera skills, but also putting his success down to his family. During the years he spent at Noravank his wife and children weren't with him, he told us, and as we paid the bill, he offered Luba and me some gentle parting advice.

'If your house is unhappy, you will have no confidence for life. An unhappy home leaves your back exposed. Success in anything comes from your entire house, never from you alone.' As he said this, gently musing out loud rather than preaching, we all fell silent for a moment with our own thoughts, scooping up some of the fallen mulberries from the table and feasting on those as well, far too good to waste.

# Summer Tolma with Barberries

A little fiddly but very worth it and much easier with practice. Think of tolma as a beginning, and call on whatever is in the refrigerator to make simple textured dishes to go alongside for meze setup: perhaps feta crumbled over a herby tomato salad, aubergines grilled with za'atar, or a crunchy cabbage and carrot salad.

**MAKES 16**

16 vine leaves in brine

100g/generous ½ cup white short-grain rice, rinsed

2 shallots, finely chopped

200g/7oz canned chopped tomatoes (plus 50g/1¾oz for the sauce)

1 tbsp tomato purée (paste)

20g/¾oz dried barberries or unsweetened dried cranberries

1 tsp sweet paprika

½ tsp ground cinnamon

¼ tsp cayenne pepper

¼ tsp ground cumin

1 tsp dried tarragon (or sage or thyme)

Handful of chopped dill and parsley

1 tbsp lemon juice

1 tbsp olive oil

½ tsp fine sea salt

½ tsp freshly ground black pepper

**FOR THE SAUCE**

2 tbsp olive oil

½ small onion, finely chopped

1 tbsp tomato purée (paste)

50g/1¾oz canned chopped tomatoes

**TO SERVE**

Thick plain yogurt

Red pepper flakes

Wash the vine leaves under hot water to rinse away the brine and set them aside while you mix the filling. Combine the rice, shallots, tomatoes, tomato purée, barberries, spices, herbs, lemon, oil and seasoning in a bowl and mix thoroughly.

Place a vine leaf on a clean surface with the stalk end toward you, vein side up. Cut off the stalk and then place about a tablespoon of rice mixture in the middle of the leaf. Bring up the sides and begin rolling, keeping it as tight and neat as possible, tucking the sides in as you go. You're looking to create as neat as possible little sausages (while tightly wrapped tolma are best, it pays not to be too precious about this process because you'll find that they hold their shape well when they're packed snugly next to one another in the pot). Continue until you have all 16 ready. If you have any mixture left, it goes well stuffed into tomatoes or bell peppers. Set the tolma aside while you make the sauce.

Select a lidded casserole dish, big enough to fit all 16 tolma in one layer and the right size and shape to accommodate a plate to hold them down when they cook; I used an 18cm/7in round casserole (capacity 1.8 litres/60fl oz). Heat the olive oil in it and cook the onion until soft with a generous pinch of fine sea salt, then add the tomato purée and the chopped tomatoes. Cook for a couple of minutes and then taste and adjust the seasoning. Remove from the heat and allow to cool.

Once the sauce is cool, put the tolma, seam side down, in a single layer on the tomato sauce, and pour in enough water to just cover them. Take a plate, a bit smaller than the pot, and that can cope with heat, or a smaller pan lid, and place it on top of the tolma to stop them rising and breaking as they cook. Simmer gently (so you don't scorch the broth) for 35–40 minutes. When ready the rice will be cooked through and soft. Serve with thick yogurt, dusted with red pepper flakes on the side.

СЕРГЕЙ ПАРА

# BLACK CAVIAR AND SMASHED PLATES – MEANDERING THROUGH PARAJANOV'S MIND

Before leaving Yerevan there was another walk I wanted to take on: a ramble through the mind of Sergei Parajanov, creative titan of the Caucasus and maestro of the film world.

It began on a quiet lane, above the dramatic Hrazdan Gorge, a sanctuary for the capital's birds. And there, in a neat courtyard belonging to Yerevan's Parajanov Museum, I joined the curator Anahit Mikayelyan. Behind the table we were seated at loomed a lifesize photographic print of Parajanov, his body behind bars, arms outstretched as if in the shape of a cross or suggesting that he might reach to take a cup of the strong Armenian coffee Mikayelyan had set before us, or one of the sweet tartlets sat glistening on a tray in the sun.

It isn't easy to neatly sum up Parajanov. An ethnic Armenian, born in Georgia in 1924 and christened as Sarkis Parajanian (his name was later Russified), he lived in Old Tbilisi with his father who sold antiques and his mother who had a fondness for wearing Christmas decorations when she gathered with her friends to sing. Tbilisi back then, with its significant Armenian population, was itself a stage set, the cultural centre of the Caucasus. Its bazaars were like theatres, rich with artistic decoration, and Art Nouveau mansions stood out with their lacy balconies, as did the dramatic rocky escarpments above the Mtkvari River.

As an adult, having survived Soviet labour camps, he lived in the Georgian capital again, entertaining friends and artists in an elaborately cluttered salon. This Tbilisian sitting room has been recreated within the museum, complete with grandfather clock, rugs, fans, jugs and pitchers, and it is so inviting that you half expect Parajanov to walk through the door at any moment, dressed in a black smock, theatrically blowing out a match, or carrying a lantern. The museum, an old house built of stone, is similar to those found in old Tbilisi today.

'My first homeland is Georgia, where I self-accomplished, the second one is Ukraine which gave me love, happiness and recognition worldwide, and my third homeland is Armenia, where my roots are and where I would like to live the rest of my life,' he once said.

Mikayelyan, who has studied his work for over a decade, stroked the floral woodblock printed tablecloth, and told me about Paravanov's generosity at his home in Tbilisi as we sipped our coffee.

'The doors were open until midnight. He was a very hospitable person, a ruler of the table, an author of gatherings.' Mikayelyan added that he liked celebrating his birthday and bringing people together for it, and how everyone remembers one particular party thrown for him in Kyiv where the whole apartment block celebrated. 'But as he had diabetes he only had a little wine. He was not a big drinker.' On his birthday every year, decades after his death, friends of the museum still gather to celebrate his life and work.

Mikayelyan passed the tray of tartlets, telling me to choose from black sesame, white sesame, barberries, saffron or chopped nuts. They were almost too pretty to eat but I took a saffron one anyway.

## LOCK-UP BOTTLE CAPS AND BLOOD-RED JUICE

Today, Parajanov is best remembered for his 1969 film *The Colour of Pomegranates*, a series of puzzling and inexplicable moving images reflecting on the life of the 18th-century Armenian lyrical poet and troubadour, Sayat-Nova. It is a dazzling cinematic experience, its originality lending a genuine timelessness. Just recently, in 2020, Lady Gaga drew heavily from it for her music video, '911', which ends with her waking up from a car crash outside a cinema where *The Colour of Pomegranates* had been showing (you can watch it on YouTube, just as millions of others have).

Parajanov planned to spend time at the Yerevan museum in his senior years; he spoke of imagining peacocks strutting as friends gathered in the courtyard where we had sat, but the project was delayed because of the devastating earthquake in the northwest of Armenia, in the winter of 1988, and he died in Yerevan of lung cancer, at midnight on 20th July 1990, just a year before the museum opened.

His spirit today lives on in these rooms. Not only are his artworks on display but everywhere there are huge portraits of him, film posters mainly. In some, he appears almost clownlike, in others regal and priestly dressed in a simple robe. But each portrait shows the same penetrating expression, the same piercing, twinkly eyes framed by heavy brows. Eyes that greet you and then follow you around.

Stepping inside the museum and into Parajanov's dreamy and flamboyant world, means entering an exciting and immediately destabilising place, one rich with folk and Christian imagery, sexual ambiguity and androgyny, all problematic themes during the Soviet era (still so now under Putin). Everywhere the eye goes, it is met with boundary-crossing art and lyric poetry converted into film and put onto canvas, or plates, or fabrics, or whatever he could use during his time in prison, often silver bottle tops. In one of the first rooms you walk through, there is a lonely-looking dining table, with just a large bowl of pomegranates at the centre, as if waiting for guests. It is breathing space before you move into the busier rooms.

As I stood before *Grandmother's Walnut Jam* (1986), a collage mixing beads, small fabric squares and buttons, I could almost taste the two black glistening preserved walnuts in a bowl. I'd seen this artwork before, at a Parajanov retrospective in Istanbul, but with Mikayelyan at my side this time, she encouraged my eyes to settle not on the walnuts but the smashed pink and white floral plate.

'The dishes and cups he used to create art were useless as they were broken but in his hands they were transformed. Damaged things, what people forget, what they throw away, he gave them new meaning. Transformation was very important to him,' Mikayelyan said as we admired the piece.

Destruction amid beauty. A chequerboard of colour and deliciousness, gone a bit awry, to be interpreted by the viewer. Just as his artworks and films were often constructed through metaphors rather than through traditional plot, character development and dialogue.

As you pass from room to room, a tableau opens up, one of coral, sea shells, wool, lace, often abstractly representing elements of his life as an incarcerated prisoner, and as a free man. Repeatedly persecuted and harassed by the Soviet authorities, and jailed on charges of homosexuality and nationalistic sentiment, *The Colour of Pomegranates* was cut, and recut, by Soviet censors, who removed or rejigged what they deemed controversial, such as religious material, while attempting to make it more understandable to Soviet film audiences, though not successfully, some critics argue.

I asked Mikayelyan about the pomegranates that feature in the film, and she told me that they 'are symbolic of the beginning of life, blood and seeds'. The fruit appears so often that trying to figure out just one meaning seems futile. In one scene, monks energetically suck the juice from pomegranates held in their hands, in another they are smashed by a sword. Film historians have dug into the possible, and questionable, nationalistic symbols in the films. The stain on a cloth, from blood-red juice spilling from a pomegranate, could shape the boundaries of the ancient Kingdom of Armenia, while the sword-smashed pomegranates may represent Sayat-Nova's death, the 1795 Iranian invasion of Tbilisi (when Sayat-Nova is widely believed to have been killed), or even the Armenian genocide.

Lavash, the bread of Armenia, also features in his films. 'Lavash has complex associations here. Each time we watch the movie, we see another thing,' Mikayelyan said. During the film, one subtitle reads, 'The bread you gave me was beautiful, but the soil is even more beautiful. I'll go soon and turn to dust. I am weary.' In another scene, a pair of angels take a folded piece of lavash stuffed with soil from the Angel of Death and give it to the poet. He embraces the bread, holding it to his heart.

Then there are eggs. During the opening scene of the film *The Legend of Suram Fortress* they are smashed. 'In old times, when they built houses and fortresses, eggs were used in building materials as they would help longevity. It was a practical thing, they used what they had,' Mikayelyan said. I remember hearing the same of old houses in Uzbekistan.

Altars as artworks are a running theme throughout the different rooms. One showcases a white marble hand, painted with small gold stars, holding an egg; another is made up of eerie wigless dolls and vintage teapots, a third holds a plastic cucumber and caviar jars. Then there is the chest of his childhood ('where it was possible to hide'), there are plates from the Kornilov Factory (St Petersburg) which Parajanov has painted with love hearts and faces. In one room, there is a narrow single bed under a huge tapestry of a young woman snoozing by a giant Caucasian shepherd dog. But of the 1,500 artworks held at the museum – assemblages, sketches made for films, hats, dolls and other personal belongings – the most striking are his collages, artworks that Parajanov considered to be concentrated films, each one dense with detail. The collages matter because, unlike his films, they were not censored. As he once said about his assemblages, they are about transfiguration, 'suitcases turn into elephants, elephants turn into suitcases'.

I walked on, into a room holding his prison masterpieces, many produced in Ukraine in the mid-1970s where he was locked up in a high security camp, or 'correctional institution'. Without tools, but with typical inspiration and adaptability, he used his fingernails to craft portraits into aluminium bottle caps made for kefir and yogurt. He referred to these as 'thalers' (the large silver coins minted in the states and territories of the Holy Roman Empire; from thaler later came the word dollar). Of prison, he was quoted once as saying: 'I am an Armenian, born in Tiflis [Tbilisi], sitting in a Russian prison for being a Ukrainian nationalist. I was in prison in Ukraine for four years and four months. Two years in other prisons. I served eight years in Tbilisi and Kiev [Kyiv]. They yelled at me, mocked and tortured me.' Ultimately, though, as these artworks prove, wherever he was locked up and mistreated, he could not be stopped.

In the spring of 1978, a matagh, or ritual sacrifice, was held at Geghard Monastery, a cultural centre of medieval Armenia, to celebrate his release from prison. But by 1982 he was arrested yet again, officially for bribing a university for his nephew's admission but really for speaking his mind at theatre discussions in Moscow. On that occasion, he was held in a dungeon at Ortachala prison in Tbilisi. A few years later, in 1985, he produced an artwork called *I Sold the Dacha*, made from postcards and photo clippings, tinsel and buttons. The dacha, just outside Tbilisi, was a gathering place and in the museum catalogue it reads 'The locals loved him dearly and attended these receptions, which were much like theatrical performances.'

A few days earlier I had walked through Yerevan's famous graveyard, Komitas Pantheon, where many of Armenia's finest artists have been laid to rest, and I'd photographed Parajanov's tomb, set with a fabulous bust, his head crowned with a wreath of pomegranates and fishes. 'Fish you see a lot in his art. It symbolises Christianity, but also represents when he was free, and not free. The fish shown in his prison drawings symbolises him during a trial, as he was silent, he could not do or say anything to help himself,' Mikayelyan said. When I spoke about visiting his grave, she added, 'to us he is still alive'.

Some have compared watching a Parajanov film to reading a novel written in hieroglyphics – beautiful but hard to decipher – but I think his films are more like fast-moving kaleidoscopes, or a huge treasure box where you uncover fantastic and unexpected things. Lovers of the avant-garde tend to revere him, as did many of his peers. 'In the temple of cinema, there are images, light, and reality. Sergei Parajanov was the master of that temple,' as the radical director of *Breathless* and *Alphaville*, Jean-Luc Godard, put it.

I left the museum and wandered back to the hotel in a stupor, my head filled with doodlings and Parajanovian things, and scenes from his complicated life: hard winters in prison, Moscow nights, a feast on the river in Tbilisi, black caviar, nut shells, dried flowers, lace, feathers, red pomegranates, thin lavash bread, smashed plates, broken cups, cigarettes, mirrors, grains of wheat, walnut jam. And a fish he'd made from various flotsam, smashed wicker chairs, bits of leather, spoons, foil, Thermos and plaster cast, a creature made three dimensional from broken things by Parajanov's hands, in order for it to come alive and swim away, free.

GALESHKA MORAVIOff PRÉSENTE UN HOMMAGE À SERGUEI PARADJA

# PARADJANOV

"Serguei Paradjanov,
pourquoi filmez-vous ?"
"Pour sanctifier
a tombe de Tarkovski."

EDITIONS COPIES NEUVES

GALESHKA MORAVIOff
Hommage
FRONTIERES

Distribué par Films Sans Fron

http://www.films-sans-frontières

ЦВЕТ ГРАНАТА

# Freekeh with Lamb and Nuts

Parajanov and pomegranates bring to mind one of the best Syrian restaurants in Yerevan, Zeituna, right by Missak Manouchian Park. There, lahmacun is served with pomegranate seeds, while freekeh (roasted cracked green durum wheat) comes with toasted nuts and lamb, a dish that reveals a delicious array of flavours and textures. I love freekeh, nutritionally superior to rice and a little smoky, and in my experience anyone who tries it for the first time wonders why they've taken so long to discover it. I also think this dish really benefits from the sweet–sour kick of pomegranate seeds and their beautiful colour.

To make this vegetarian, keep the nuts but swap out the lamb for crumbled feta and top with plenty of chopped soft herbs. For both versions, I also like a couple of hot pickled peppers on the side.

**SERVES 2 GENEROUSLY**

**FOR THE FREEKEH**

3 tbsp olive oil

½ red onion, finely chopped

1 garlic clove, sliced

A couple of thyme sprigs

200g/7oz freekeh, well rinsed and drained

50ml/3 tbsp white wine

350ml/1½ cups vegetable stock

**FOR THE LAMB AND NUT TOPPING**

1 garlic clove, sliced

½ tsp cumin seeds

150g/5½oz diced lamb shoulder

½ tsp fine sea salt

70g/2½oz mixed nuts: pine nuts, cashews, whole blanched almonds

Small handful of soft herbs, preferably mint and coriander (cilantro)

Handful of pomegranate seeds

Put a large, lidded, heavy-based pan or casserole over a moderate heat, pour in 2 tablespoons of the oil and add the onion, then cook until soft and glossy. Add the garlic and cook for 2 more minutes, then add the thyme and cook for a further minute. Tip in the freekeh, the wine and stock, put the lid on and cook over a low heat, stirring from time to time, for 25–30 minutes. Remove from the heat but leave the lid on to steam while you prepare the nuts and lamb.

Heat the remaining oil in a frying pan until hot, add the garlic and cook just until the pungency lessens, then briefly fry the cumin seeds. Add the lamb and season with ½ teaspoon of salt then fry the meat over a medium heat, until browned. Remove with a slotted spoon (leaving the oil in the pan) and keep it warm under foil. Add the nuts to the pan and fry until they have plenty of colour.

To serve, shape the freekeh into a neat round with a hollow to hold the nuts, then scatter the pieces of lamb onto the nuts. Top with some finely chopped soft herbs and perhaps some pomegranate seeds.

# Green Olive Lahmacun

How promising can a café be if you enter it via a touristy trinket shop? If it is Abovyan 12, a courtyard restaurant in downtown Yerevan, then the answer is 'surprisingly so'. Passing through the shop and into the restaurant, vines climb and twist skywards ensuring that the tables, covered in red and black cloths, similar to Scottish Laronde tartan, are kept shaded. Above, up some steps, is an art gallery displaying Parajanovian-style paintings and collages. It isn't hard to imagine the maestro himself dining somewhere like this, holding court in a shadowy corner.

In the centre of the courtyard, a tap constantly runs into a basin holding shiny watermelons, the sound itself cooling, while on the menu you'll find spas (yogurt soup), almost half the price of all other soups as it is an essential hot-weather remedy. As well as spas, at Abovyan 12 I like to order their simple olive lahmacun, which is wildly popular in Armenia and also easy to make at home.

## MAKES 2 LARGE LAHMACUN

**For the dough**

250g/1¾ cups strong white bread flour, plus extra for dusting

1 tsp fine salt

7g/¼oz dried fast-action yeast

1 tbsp vegetable oil

Cornmeal or semolina flour, for dusting

**FOR THE TOPPING**

260g/9¼oz pitted green olives, chopped as small as possible

2 tbsp olive oil, plus extra for drizzling

5 tbsp tomato purée (paste)

2 garlic cloves, peeled and crushed

1 small red onion, finely chopped

¼ tsp red pepper flakes

¼ tsp ground cumin

¼ tsp freshly ground black pepper

¼ fine salt

¼ tsp ground allspice

Juice of ½ lemon

A small bunch of flat-leaf parsley, finely chopped, to serve

Put the flour into a large bowl and add the salt to one side and the yeast to the other. Make a well in the middle and slowly pour in 190ml/¾ cup of water, followed by the oil, and combine to a dough. On a lightly floured surface, knead the dough for 10 minutes until the tackiness has gone, adding a little more flour if you need to. Place in a lightly oiled bowl, cover with a damp tea towel and leave to rise in a warm place until doubled in size, about 30 minutes.

Combine the chopped olives with 1 tablespoon of olive oil in a bowl. Set aside. In another bowl, combine the remaining ingredients except the parsley.

Preheat the oven to its maximum temperature and dust 2 large baking trays thinly with cornmeal or semolina flour.

Briefly knead the risen dough, then split it in two. Roll each half out into a large thin circle, about 30cm/12in diameter, and place them on the prepared baking trays. Using the back of a spoon, spread a very thin layer of the tomato topping, then scatter the chopped olives evenly on top. Bake for 15–20 minutes or until crispy around the edges (you may want to turn the trays once, depending on your oven) and drizzle over a little more olive oil before serving hot, scattered with parsley.

# Omelette with Dates

The origins of this dish are Iranian but as Iran has long had an Armenian community it is possible to find it on menus in Yerevan, including at the courtyard café Abovyan 12, which is where I first tried it for breakfast. A date omelette, a glass of ice-cold Jermuk and hot black coffee. Why not? It works so well. Sweet, but not sugary sweet, light but filling, good all year round.

**MAKES 1**

3 pitted dates

2 large eggs, beaten

Pinch of sea salt and freshly ground black pepper

Light grating of nutmeg

¼ tsp red pepper flakes

1 tsp vegetable oil

5g/1 tsp butter

A few coriander (cilantro) leaves, to garnish

Put the dates into a bowl and pour over just enough boiling water to cover and let them soften for 5 minutes. When cool enough to handle, chop into small pieces.

Season the beaten eggs with salt, pepper and the spices (keep a few red pepper flakes back to sprinkle over at the end). Heat the oil and butter in a non-stick frying pan over a medium-low heat until the butter has melted and is foaming. Pour the eggs into the frying pan and let the mixture cook for 30 seconds then scatter over the dates and cook until the egg has just set. Fold in half with a spatula. Garnish with the coriander leaves, reserved pepper flakes, extra salt and pepper, and serve with flatbreads.

# A DINING ROOM AT THE WRITERS' HOUSE

Rammed relentlessly by the midsummer sun, eventually the thing to do in Yerevan is to leave. Lake Sevan beckoned. Given that it is freshwater and at high altitude, and therefore cooler, how could it not?

And it wasn't just the lake that summoned, but also the Sevan Writers' House, a futuristic architectural masterpiece built decades ago that today operates as a hotel. I'd seen a photograph of it in a book, one part of it, with the dining room, shaped like a giant snowshoe, balanced on a single thick concrete leg, jutting out from a rock face. Jean-Paul Sartre and Simone de Beauvoir had stayed once, arriving by car from neighbouring Georgia. Later, de Beauvoir described the landscape surrounding Sevan as 'a pinkish, chaotic desert with a bright blue lake in the middle of it'.

Having been holed up in the city with the weather dominating the conversation – 'how much hotter can it possibly get?', 'who can even *think* in this heat?' – we were keen to get out. But that isn't to suggest that we were down on Yerevan, not in the slightest.

Driving out of the city, concentration and self-confidence were essential. Drivers had a tendency to overtake, and undertake, sharply, taking advantage of any signs of hesitation. But once away from the tangled insect crawl of bashed-up vehicles, the roads were easier, more forgiving, and quickly we indulged a sensation of adventure. Feeling liberated, we wound the windows all the way down, then veering off a main road onto a smaller unsealed artery we took on a high plateau, quickly finding ourselves entirely alone with only the purr of the engine and the buzzing of insects surrounding us. We were on the open road, with all the time in the world and zero pressure, and the sat nav we'd hired was working well. The brilliant sun pummelled the plains that stretched out for as far as we could see, halted only by tawny-tinted hills. Despite only travelling for just over an hour, suddenly, Yerevan felt very far away.

'Let's stop and take a photo,' I innocently suggested. This turned out to be a mistake.

James switched off the engine. We sipped water, got out, stretched and photographed the surroundings. The car windows, I noticed, were no longer shiny and clear but speckled with sticky dead insects. Overheating quickly, we got back into the shade of the Lada, keen to move, to have the breeze blow through the windows again, but when James tried to start the ignition, nothing happened. Literally no pull or kick. Nothing at all.

'Oh dear,' he said.

Nervous heave of the stomach. Just one truck had passed us since we'd stopped. The strongest imaginable light fell all around us, dazzling and golden. How long might we be stranded?

James got out and propped open the bonnet for a look, sat back down, tried the engine with no luck, then repeated it all again. After half an hour or so, another Lada, almost identical to ours, stopped. Two middle-aged men, both dressed in short-sleeved polo shirts, opened their car doors, got out, lit cigarettes, and moved James aside. The benefit to hiring a Lada is a common shared knowledge among drivers about their quirks and workings. Ladas are utilitarian. They may be Russian-made but they are Armenia's national car. Fruit is sold out of their boots, rugs for sale are draped over them, people lean on them for hours, chatting and smoking. One of the men got into the driving seat.

'Barev dzez' (hello) we said to one another politely. The man turned the key. Nothing. A suck of the teeth. Another attempt. Again, nothing. After some head-scratching, he returned with James and they took it in turns to try and finally the car juddered into action. A knack was needed, nothing more. Let the car cool down a bit and start it up slowly, the man explained to James in Russian. Thanks followed then the shaking of hands and slaps on the back, and then we were off again. I patted my forehead with a dissolving tissue.

We were heading north towards the lake, confidence restored and the frequency for a local radio station found.

'The guidebook says that Noratus is very nearby, you know the famous field of khachkars? Can't we stop there for a while?' I asked James at the wheel. He sighed and reluctantly agreed; after all it was a short detour.

We drove in slowly, passing other Ladas belonging to Armenian visitors who had parked up.

'You get out and walk, I'll keep the engine going to be on the safe side,' said James.

I stepped out of the car. Nothing can quite prepare you for the old cemetery of Noratus. Almost a thousand priceless khachkars, some dating back to the 10th century, scattered in scrubby grassland where unexpected flocks of sheep graze among them. At the first few, I crouched down and saw that they were carved with expressive human faces, almost cartoon-like, and like all the others were decorated with complex geometric carvings. The sun lit up the lichens that covered them, forming lacelike mosaics in colours of rust, cream, lime and pistachio green.

Some believe that the cultural origins of khachkars are connected to the beginnings of Christianity in Armenia in the 4th century, when sandstone imagery carved into stone slabs was more likely to appeal to an illiterate populace than Christ on the cross. Some were raised as tombstones or memorials but others were built purely for their own exquisite beauty. The British Museum has one, from the 13th century, though not currently on show. However, on display at New York City's Metropolitan Museum of Art is an even earlier one (12th century) from northern Armenia. The grand Armenian cathedral in Lviv, western Ukraine, has several khachkars in its grounds. Given the size of the Armenian diaspora – seven million or so – mainly living in the US, Russia and France, compared to the three million living in Armenia itself, khachkars can be found in many places where Armenians have settled. They remind me of ancient cross stones in Scotland, featuring symbols of the Picts, the ancient Celtic people who roamed north of the River Clyde in the Early Middle Ages.

It would have taken several hours to tour the huge site in detail so as the sun kept beating down, the lake, and the promise of its sunset, pulled at us to get going.

To exit, we drove past a modern cemetery on the outskirts of old Noratus decorated with Armenian flags flying by graves newly dug for soldiers killed in the fighting in Nagorno-Karabakh. Artyom, a grave digger we stopped to speak to, explained that it costs ten thousand dollars for a bespoke gravestone like the elaborate gilded ones he stood by. Each tombstone was decorated with a double portrait depicting a young man: etched on one side, the deceased appearing in civilian clothes, on the other dressed in his army uniform. All around us biblical-looking wheat fields formed a backdrop.

Back on the road soon enough Lake Sevan came into distant view, shimmering like blue satin, then, as we got closer, so did all the provisions and facilities that exist to serve the lake-goers: shacks refurbished as takeaway cafés, beach resorts, shashlik vendors, paddle boats for rent and pop-up beer bars. We continued until the Writers' House appeared, unmistakably, with little fanfare or signage. Its two striking buildings, so different from each other, were advertisement enough. We were glad to finally have arrived at the Sevan Creativity House of the Writers' Union of Armenia, to give it its full name, and with plenty of time, we hoped, for dinner. Having parked right under the concrete stilt holding the building up, it was immediately clear that this magnificent lakeside hideaway was in urgent need of repair but it was still thrilling to be there. The original hotel block sits tucked behind the heaving modernist building that the resort is famous for. How it came together as one complex, over several decades, tells the troubling story of its architects, Gevorg Kochar and Mikayel Mazmanyan.

At the entrance to the giant lounge building, the manager came out to greet us, a tall, large, blue-eyed and quiet man, he spread his arms wide to welcome us, with the words 'Soviet modernism', and, seemingly happy that we'd be spending the night, handed me a key for room number one. On the wall behind him were photographs of the original architectural sketches for the 1960s building we stood in. Pointing to the older building, the residence hall with its semicircle balconies, the manager explained that that was where we'd sleep. He then ushered us into the main curved dining room, with panoramic floor-to-ceiling windows perfectly framing the lake, white drapes billowing, the warm air of the room smelling of dust, fruit, beer and roses. We cooed again and again. The room, with its wooden flooring, almost certainly original, and the view, were both spectacular.

In the mid-1930s, the residence hall, or hotel, set on a rocky slope facing Lake Sevan, was completed with a kitchen, billiard room, dining hall and a bathroom serving each floor. At that time of the Soviet Union, leisure resorts and sanatoriums were being rapidly constructed to provide workers with the opportunity to rest and recover in scenic locations. But this was also when independent artistic associations were banned and unions were established instead such as the Union of Writers, along with their accompanying 'Creativity Houses'. Disaster came in 1937 when, just two years after the completion of the hotel, its architects Kochar and Mazmanyan were arrested, accused of sabotage against the Soviet Union, and deported to Krasnoyarsk Krai in Russia. It wasn't until 1954, shortly after the death of Stalin, that they were released. In 1963, another floor to the Residence Hall was added, with a sun deck and clubroom, and a separate 'lounge building' with its visionary design and huge lake views came to fruition. After the USSR collapsed in 1991, the Writers' Union kept the Sevan resort operating for its original purpose, though anyone, not only writers, can book a room today.

Stepping out onto the curved balcony, we each pulled up a seat and breathed in the cooler air, the lake glittering far below, silvery and alluring. We opened a bottle of wine we'd carried with us from Vayots Dzor, heavy and heady, all red berry flavours and peppery notes, and tasting of the rocky volcanic soil from where it had come, and I thought of the famous William S. Burroughs quote: 'Perhaps all pleasure is only relief.' Finally, I was cool and comfortable for the first time in weeks.

The lake had captivated the brilliant poet Osip Mandelstam who had visited Armenia for several inspiring months in 1930. On Lake Sevan, he looked out and saw a tantalising, long-gone, spectacle: 'Daily at five o'clock on the dot, the lake, which teems with trout, would boil up as though a huge pinch of soda had been thrown into it.'

Mandelstam found his poetic voice again in Armenia. He reads the land, tries to learn the language and, developing an 'Ararat sense', notes the Armenian connections to the earth and clay, like the pottery of ancient Greece, singling out the ceramics as, 'A beautiful land's hollow book' and in a poem from 1930: 'Azure and clay, clay and azure', bringing to mind the lake. He revels in it, and is resurrected by the country. 'When you look around, your eyes need more salt. You catch forms and colours – and it is all unleavened bread. Such is Armenia.'

By Lake Sevan, he described walking through hip-height grass, and being almost blinded by red poppies, 'Bright to the point of surgical pain … Fire in my hands, as if a blacksmith had lent me some coals.'

Four years later he was arrested for an epigram he'd written about Stalin, a 'sixteen-line death sentence' as it has been called, and four years after that the government reported that Mandelstam had died of heart failure, though it is believed he died of typhoid in a gulag near Vladivostok.

Back in the dining room, where tables had been laid with cloths of a pomegranate design, all was silent once a group of young touring Armenian artists, armed with a portable stereo, had stubbed out their cigarettes and left. As the only overnight guests, we were installed at one of the tables for dinner, the air heavily weighted with the smell of fried fish, delicious little whole trout from the lake, served through a hatch from a kitchen at the back of the dining hall. Plates of fresh herbs came to the table, too, along with lavash bread. We drank Armenian Ararat brandy as it got dark, and icy Jermuk sparkling water, of course, feeling immensely nourished not only by the flavours but the hospitality, the ingenious design and history of the remarkable building.

The next day, we'd take a short walk to the Sevanavank Monastery located on the peninsula, literally just behind us (and one of the most visited because of its convenient lakeside location) but for that moment, we simply enjoyed the atmosphere. Relishing the delights of a homemade dinner as through the open balcony doors came the most delicious cool breeze.

# Aubergine and Yogurt Dip

Excellent for a shared table and based on a side dish I ate at the restaurant belonging to the Tufenkian Avan Marak Tsapatagh Hotel near the shores of Lake Sevan. In Armenia, this would be made with thick yogurt called madzoon, or matsoni in Georgia, which, some say, takes its name from the old Armenian word mats (to curdle). With a little caution, you can be as creative here as you like, adding pistachios, pine nuts or chopped hazelnuts, different leafy herbs, while turning up or down the heat from the red pepper flakes.

**SERVES 4 AS PART OF A MEZE PLATTER**

1 large aubergine (eggplant)

1 large garlic clove

2 tbsp olive oil (save a little for swirling)

1 tbsp lemon juice

125g/generous ½ cup natural yogurt

Sea salt flakes and black pepper, to taste

50g/1¾oz blanched almonds, toasted

½ tsp red pepper flakes

A few fresh mint leaves

If you have a gas burner, place the aubergine over the flame and turn with tongs until its skin is flaky and blackened and the inside is silky and cooked. If not, turn your oven grill to high, cut the aubergine in half lengthways, make a few holes in the skin with a knife, rub with a little oil, season and grill, skin side up, until blistered and then turn over and cook the flesh side until soft (test with a knife).

When it is cool enough to handle, discard the skin then blitz the aubergine flesh in a food processor, throwing in the garlic clove to mince with it and pouring in a little more oil as you go. Transfer to a serving bowl, mixing through the remaining oil, lemon juice, yogurt and salt and pepper to taste. Scatter over the almonds, red pepper flakes and mint leaves and serve at once (otherwise keep refrigerated but serve at room temperature).

# Gata with Apricots and Nuts

Before we left the Writers' House, to head northwest to the city of Gyumri, I made time for a coffee and a slice of gata on the balcony of the dining room, the lake stretching out below. Gata is a bread-like cake, and it is for you if you like, say, half and half popcorn, because it is as salty as it is sweet. In Armenia, it is especially linked to Geghard Monastery where vendors have displayed, and sold, gata for as long as anyone can remember. Cook, writer and baking specialist Andrew Janjigian has written beautifully, and in depth, about gata for the Serious Eats website; do look him up if you are interested.

For this particular gata I used a variety of seeds – any mixture of the following works well: pumpkin, sunflower, sesame, brown linseed.

**SERVES 6–8**

**FOR THE DOUGH**

70g/⅓ cup caster (superfine) sugar

80g/⅓ cup unsalted butter, softened

1½ tsp fine salt

160g/¾ cup Greek yogurt

1 egg

280g/2¼ cups plain (all-purpose) flour, plus extra for dusting

7g/¼oz fast-action dried yeast

¼ tsp bicarbonate of soda (baking soda)

**FOR THE FILLING**

40g/3 tbsp unsalted butter, melted

50g/1¾oz toasted walnuts, chopped into pea-size pieces

40g/1½oz dried unsulphured apricots, chopped into pea-size pieces

20g/¾oz mixed seeds, toasted

2 tbsp plain (all-purpose) flour

¼ tsp fine salt

¼ tsp almond extract

1 egg, beaten, to glaze

In a large mixing bowl, cream the sugar and butter together. Add the salt, yogurt and egg and stir to combine, then tip in the flour, yeast and bicarbonate of soda (baking soda). Bring it together as best you can (it will be a little sticky), adding a little more flour if necessary, and then tip out onto a clean surface and knead a few times until the stickiness is gone.

Flatten the dough out into a round disc about 22cm/8½in and put onto a dinner plate. Let it rest, covered, at room temperature for 25 minutes and then transfer to the refrigerator to chill for 1 hour.

Meanwhile, make the filling. Add all the ingredients to a bowl, apart from the egg and combine well with a spoon to form a nubbly paste.

Preheat the oven to 200°C/400°F/gas mark 6 and line a baking tray with parchment paper. Remove the dough from the refrigerator, roll it out into a thick

25cm/10in disc and put the filling in the middle, leaving at least 5cm/2in clear from the edge.

Now you need to assemble the gata. Bring the sides up, gradually folding into the centre, making a money bag shape, until the filling is covered with dough. Flatten it shut using your palm, then turn over onto the baking sheet so the sealed side is underneath. You should have a round about 15cm/6in diameter. Gata are usually decorated, and I use the back of a fork to make some criss-cross lines (though once baked they do tend to disappear a little).

Lastly, glaze well with the beaten egg and bake for 25–30 minutes or until deeply golden all over. Allow to cool before serving.

# PILGRIMAGE TO A MARBLE MONASTERY

By this point, I'd luxuriated in trying many specialities of Armenia from jingalov hats to arishta but I'd abstained from the dish I longed for most, thinking of it regularly but waiting patiently for it, because I needed it to be just right.

Trout lavash is a simple meal in one, but it demands immediacy. All must be fresh as fresh can be: grilled trout that has not travelled far, herbs that are spry, and just-baked paper-thin lavash. The fish-centric restaurant Cherkezi Dzor, in Gyumri, Armenia's second city, had all the necessary pieces in place: a well-regarded onsite fish farm with ample good water, and local flour, sourced from the surrounding valleys of Shirak, for making the bread.

As night fell, people packed into this indoors–outdoors space, set in a ravine away from the centre of town, with everything carved from wood to reflect the surroundings and with gardens ringed by artificial lakes. But there was something peculiar, too, something heavy and unexpected about this sought-after restaurant: we diners were overlooked by towers and soldiers belonging to the Russian 102nd Military Base. Russians built fortresses in Gyumri in the 19th century, when the city was known as Alexandropol (later, in the Soviet era, it became Leninakan) and Gyumri, concerned for its borders, has long hosted several thousand troops though the continued need for a Russian military presence in Armenia is debated.

When the trout lavash arrived, rolled up like a wrap, along with a side salad very lightly dressed with lemon juice and olive oil, I knew it had been worth the wait. The trout was plump and juicy and the bread soft and warm as velvet and blistered all over and, within its layers, there was butter and sour cream and maybe dill and definitely tarragon. I ate it unapologetically fast, spurred on by its deliciousness and my hunger which had been made strong by the day's hot and trying walk. Ordering another beer, we recounted the trip while occasionally casting an eye up to the army watchtowers.

### SHOE-SUCKING BOGS AND HIGH-RISK HOGWEED

From the hot back streets of downtown Gyumri, lined with cherry trees and tsarist-era houses, all iron work and peeling paint, we'd set off to walk to Marmashen Monastery. With no map, just instructions from a friend to 'follow the Akhuryan river', once we'd left the city limits behind we began by walking northwest, very near to the (closed) Turkish border, with the green military fortress and its Russian flags close by.

As we approached the water, small flies flitted in front of my eyes like tiny stars. A constant pest, they were swarming because of the reeking dung from a ginormous herd of cows clustering around the banks of the river, which was also teeming with white egrets. The cows, we realised, were with calves and that was a problem. If you've ever lived in sheep-farming country, as I have (in North Yorkshire), you know to avoid them, especially if they're with their young, as occasionally, more often than you might think, cows get spooked and trample, sometimes to death, walkers, especially those with dogs. We edged away and began embarking upon a huge loop to avoid them.

Cows were not the only threat close to the water's edge. Masses of giant hogweed sprouted skywards. A type of fast-spreading cow parsley, with clusters of white flowers on bushy bristly stems, giant hogweed looks harmless but it is rightly demonised. If human skin merely brushes it the result is often terrible blisters and severe skin burns. An invasive species, in the past it was introduced to Europe from the western Caucasus though most gardeners now, aware of its high risks, want it eradicated. Looping around the drove of cows and hogweed meant going over expanses of shoe-sucking bogs and large puddles from which leapt countless frogs. Often finding ourselves marooned on dry patches trying to find a way forward, we pushed on as best we could, drinking Jermuk and snacking on salty pretzel sticks, treading over the swampy ground, various amphibians leaping over boots as we went. It took a couple of hours just to go a few kilometres.

Because of the flies, and my hands that were swatting at them again and again thus blurring the countryside, I couldn't be sure at first of what it was that flew past me. But there it was again with its distinctive stripes. Another step, and it zoomed closer. Finally, I caught a proper look: long bill curving downwards and a large fantastic crest. A hoopoe, no doubt about it. A common sight to many but not to you if you've never seen one. I was so struck by the sight of such an unexpected and majestic bird that I said out loud, 'A hoopoe, a hoopoe …!' Then, I saw it one last time, as it went off heading behind a large rock, wingbeats slow and bounding. It more than made up for the detour, heat, flies, hogweed and mud. Even when things go wrong on a walk, there are always rewards, waiting, just there, just up ahead.

Wandering ever further from the riverbank we eventually came to the village of Marmashen where two men were busy having a fist fight outside the village shop. Very little else, though, seemed to be happening, just a few farmers tending to their cabbage and potato crops while tiny newborn calves lolled in fields and lizards darted along walls.

The monastery, unusual in that it is set in a valley rather than an elevated position, still couldn't be seen. We asked a couple of residents if there was a track to it, assuming that both the village and church must have been there before the arrival of cars and that worshippers would have once walked, but we were told no, the only way was to follow the road, which sent us again in the wrong direction.

### STRAYED FROM THE RIVER

Despite the bucolic scenery, I cursed that our route had failed. We were lost. Not badly lost, but lost. What was supposed to be an easy river stroll of about three hours, taking into account the sun, had now morphed into a slog. By avoiding the cows, we'd been forced into a string of small lanes which had led to the village and detoured us from the simple 'follow the river' route. I cursed the cows, cursed the patchy phone signal, then cursed my bites too. I had been bitten from feet to knees by either mosquitoes or bedbugs and, learning of a trick from a chemist in Gyumri, had begun rubbing cinnamon oil onto my legs every night to avoid more. The sickly-sweet smell haunted my nostrils.

We walked out onto the sun-drenched main road which we pounded for another three or four kilometres or so. 'Stupid not to have a map,' I muttered, looking up at the hills surrounding the valley where huge white crosses had been carved, or painted. The cross made me think of Komitas Vardapet, Armenia's saintly scholar-singer who has come to symbolise Armenian sacred music, as well as the country's shared national resilience. In Turkey, almost visible from where we walked, he had established a 300-member choir, but it was there, in April 1915 that he, along with other intelligentsia of the Armenian community of Constantinople, was arrested and deported to Çankırı, close to Ankara. Komitas was brutalised but survived. Suffering seriously from post-traumatic stress disorder, and rendered mute by his experiences, he spent many years in French asylums, broken by the ordeal.

Finally, as we rounded a corner, we became certain that we were on the right track as there were suddenly more cars on the road suggesting other visitors en route to the famous monastery. But the cars stoked another fear: how to get back? I didn't want a return trek through the boggy fields, past the cows, feet heavy from boots clogged with thick mud. Maybe we'd hitchhike, I thought, as we peered inside a tiny roadside church. The room was little bigger than a broom cupboard yet it was full of deities of Jesus, each one similar and many lined up against the sunny windowsill.

The long winding road from the little church grew dustier, and the complex we aimed for remained tantalisingly out of sight. Then, just as the last sparks of enjoyment of the walk began to entirely sap away, conical roofs, elegant cupolas and cylindrical drums suddenly appeared. We were almost there.

Once the burial place for the Armenian noble Pahlavuni dynasty, Marmashen was consecrated in 1029 and plundered by the Seljuks in 1064. And now? Curiously, dance music was coming from speakers where a group of teenagers were dancing in a nearby dell. A weekend gathering. Descending into the valley, filled with apple trees, we walked towards it, newly energised by relief. At the monastery were saffron-coloured khachkars decorated with bunches of grapes, baked in the sun, while past the doorway (where someone had left a little rug and a cup of coffee) inside, people were making the cross, admiring the multicoloured icons, and lighting candles by faded frescoes of Bible scenes. It was hard to see why it is known as 'the marble monastery', because while the site's unusual name, Marmashen, comes from the word for marble, it was built from local orange tuff.

Mission to Marmashen complete, we managed to arrange a taxi back to Gyumri, by calling a local number that another pilgrim had passed on to us written on a scrap of paper. And as soon as we returned, I looked up the Eurasian Hoopoe, wanting to confirm what I'd seen. Sometimes spotted strutting about with its crest fanned, it is a common bird in Armenia apparently but not, according to *The Field Guide to the Birds of Armenia*, where I'd noticed it, there, by the river. At that location it is 'expected to be seen on less than five per cent' of birdwatching field trips. The walk had, for entirely unexpected reasons, been worth it.

# Eetch – Bulgur Wheat Salad

A deeply refreshing meal that is ideal after a hot walk. Eetch is essentially fine bulgur infused with tomato juice, not entirely dissimilar to tabbouleh though with a different, less dry, consistency. The herb and spring onion topping is the secret here: leave it out and the eetch will seem flat. Serve as part of a wider spread of dishes alongside lavash or other flatbread.

**SERVES 4 AS A SIDE OR PART OF A MEZE PLATTER**

2 tbsp olive oil

2 small onions, grated

1½ tsp sea salt

¼ tsp freshly ground black pepper

1 large red bell pepper, finely chopped

1 garlic clove, minced

½ tsp paprika

½ tsp red pepper flakes

45g/1½oz double-concentrated tomato purée (paste)

225g/8oz canned chopped tomatoes

Juice of ½ lemon

180g/6¼oz fine bulgur wheat

360ml/1½ cups plus 1 tbsp boiling water

**FOR THE TOPPING**

2 small spring onions (scallions), finely chopped

Handful of fresh herbs (a mix of curly parsley, basil, dill, mint), finely chopped

1 tbsp lemon juice

1 tbsp extra-virgin olive oil

Heat the olive oil in a large saucepan, then add the onion, salt, black pepper and half the chopped bell pepper, cooking until soft. Briefly cook the garlic until the pungency lessens. Add the spices, tomato purée, chopped tomatoes and lemon juice and cook for 5 minutes. Next, tip in the bulgur, coating well with the tomato mixture, then pour over the boiling water. Stir everything together, cover the pan, and allow to simmer over a very low heat for 5 minutes (check it isn't sticking to the bottom of the pan, if so gently stir). Then turn off the heat and let it steam, with the lid on, for another 10 minutes. Remove from the heat. Allow to cool completely, then transfer into a serving bowl and refrigerate. When ready to serve, remove from the fridge and allow to come to room temperature, then garnish with the remaining chopped bell pepper, the spring onions and herbs. Dress with the lemon juice and olive oil.

# THE DYNAMIC ABUNDANCE OF THE ASLAMAZYAN SISTERS

Beckoning like a giant yawning mouth, a shadowy archway crafted from black stone leads into 242 Abovyan Street, a grand imperial mansion built in Gyumri in 1880. Of all the tsarist-era buildings, survivors of the terrible 1988 earthquake, this is one of the most bewitching. At its centre sits a well-tended rose-filled courtyard, the soft floral scent of anise, cloves and honeysuckle all around, framed skywards with surrounding latticed wooden balconies, the sort an aria might be sung from. The mansion is somehow operatic both in how it feels and how it looks, setting high expectations. But this expressive and dramatic exterior perfectly rings in its subject: two artists, two women artists, the sisters Mariam and Yeranuhi Aslamazyan.

Painting for half a century, from the 1940s to the 90s, the Aslamazyan sisters were versatile, producing travel sketches, still lifes, ceramics and portraits. They were both physically striking, too, often photographed in beautiful robes. Mariam especially, with her strong poise and presence, dressed in bright clothes and heavy jewellery, black hair in a centre parting tied back in a bun, a look that has led many to describe her, somewhat lazily, as the Armenian Frida Kahlo. Better, I think, was the characterisation given by the art critic Lilit Sargsyan who refers to her as 'the "Amazon of the Sixties" – one of the brightest stars in their magnificent galaxy.' Famous sibling painters aren't that common (the Chapman brothers, Georgia O'Keeffe and her sister Ida, to name two) which adds, I think, to their mystique, appeal and brand.

Born into a large family, who built their wealth through the development of water mills in Armenia and Georgia, the Aslamazyans lived in comfort in the village of Bash-Shirak, close to Gyumri, the very last outpost before the Turkish border. That was until the Soviets came to power and Bolshevik authorities confiscated the family's property, quickly transforming them from rich to poor.

The sisters, Armenian by blood and heritage, later became glorified painters of the Soviet Union, to which they showed, at least outwardly, loyalty, despite it being the same system that had crushed their family. They are remembered for being exemplary women artists, and they were.

Studying in Soviet Russia was hard as daughters of a wealthy Armenian family. Mariam was initially deprived of a scholarship and Yeranuhi tried to get on in Moscow but moved back to Yerevan. Mariam, desperate to study, enlisted the help of Nadezhda Krupskaya, widow of Lenin, who agreed that she should not suffer for the 'sins' of her family, and helped her to gain entry to the competitive Vkhutemas technical art school. Yeranuhi's artistic education took her to Kharkiv, in Ukraine, then back to Russia, to the Leningrad Academy of Fine Arts where Mariam joined her. By the end of the 1930s, they were both members of the Leningrad Union of Painters.

With the USSR so ardently supporting their work, they were swept up by it, taking trips sponsored by Soviet officialdom to paint in countries such as Madagascar, Japan and Egypt, to promote their art as well as the regime. In India, Mariam was awarded the Jawaharlal Nehru prize for strengthening Indian–Soviet friendship. 'One could spend a lifetime in India, so attractive is this country. But a lifetime would not be enough …' Mariam said in 1971.

During the Second World War they turned their attention, and paintbrushes, to war, Mariam going so far as to produce socialist realism propaganda posters encouraging people to fight, and painting portraits of Stalin and Lenin. But in diaries and memoirs, as Armenian art historians are keen to point out, Mariam expressed, cautiously, her fears about authorities cracking down on artists. The unfairness of it all. It was a dedication to their craft that helped them survive. And though they lived in Russia, it was to Armenia they'd return for artistic inspiration.

Today at the museum in Gyumri, Yeranuhi's work is on the first floor, Mariam's on the second. One still life, *The Window of the Studio* (1973), by Yeranuhi depicts a windowsill with bottles and an elegant candlestick and a little string of wooden camels and a donkey. Simple but convincing and enticing, it works because it feels like looking into a private space. In many works there are sun-drenched stripes, influences of local textiles, and running motifs of masks, pomegranates, grapes and poppies. Kitchen pitchers, jugs and rugs. 'After a series of difficult experiences I began to value the pleasures of life. By painting I admired the nature of my motherland, the free spirit of my nation, and sweet fruits,' Mariam is quoted as saying in the museum catalogue.

On the upper floor, one of Mariam's paintings, *Peppers, Flame* (1978), stands out as a visual punch. Hanging on strings, in this oil-on-canvas ode to peppers, are yellow ones, green ones, orange ones and, mostly, red ones. Dozens of them, replayed, until the whole canvas is covered. One pepper, burning bright and filled with energy, is the entry point for the viewer to another as they repeat and repeat until all you see is an inviting glossy mass. The tempo of the painting is hot and fast but also true to nature. There is little room to breathe when looking at it, yet you want, more than anything, to sink your teeth into the smooth skins.

Looking at the painting is not only to consume Armenian culture, but to eat up the fresh peppers, and to devour them with wonder, as if we are seeing them, and tasting them, for the first time. The overall brightness could represent a longing for flavour, for sun, for colour, for home. Or love. In the catalogue, *Peppers, Flame* is described as 'sensual, scorching, striking with simplicity and at the same time, with the utmost veracity … the peppers cease to be vegetables but rather turn into hieroglyphs.' Painted with such sure-footedness, Mariam's vision and curiosity for the peppers fires ours as the viewer, making it an easy artwork to remember, which is part of its star quality.

And yet. How can we know what was really going on in her mind when she painted them? The colour red that dominates the painting is also the colour of danger, of attention. The colour of the Red Guards, the star that represents the Communist Party, the colour of blood, fire and combat. There is passion in the shine but also there is danger in the lividness and heat. Could the painting be a warning? How the fruits of the earth are disrupted by sickness and war?

Over the decades, many Aslamazyan artworks had been absorbed into the halls of Russia's galleries, which has in its collective vaults much art from across the Caucasus. Moscow's State Tretyakov Gallery has celebrated Mariam's work with solo shows in the past and the director of the city's State Museum of Oriental Art,

Alexander Sedov, once described Mariam as being 'saturated with talent' though in his museum most of her work is not on permanent display, and is therefore, sadly, hidden from view.

By the time the museum in Gyumri opened in the 1980s, the sisters had donated much of their art, more than six hundred pieces, back to the city from Russia. But it was unfortunate timing. Shortly after they did so, the 1988 earthquake struck and the museum became a transitory home for the desperate and displaced, not reopening to visitors until 2005.

It occurred to me, flicking through the catalogue that I brought home, that other still-life paintings of fruit and vegetables – *Pumpkins on Woollen Plaid* (1944), *Still Life, Oranges* (1954) and *Fruit from Sukhumi* (1959) – are now concealed in more ways than one. Not only are they not on display but they are cut adrift in Russia, a country that is now sealed off from most of us, as its barbaric full-scale invasion of Ukraine continues. It is unnerving, but also entirely obvious, that the Soviet mindset, the imperial mindset, is somehow controlling the Aslamazyan sisters' work even today, after their deaths. And not only that. Death has also forever parted the two sisters by several hundred miles. Mariam was buried in Yerevan, at the grand Komitas Pantheon, but Yeranuhi was laid to rest at the Armenian Cemetery in Moscow.

Երանուհի Ասլամազյան Eranuhi Aslamazyan
74 Best Still Life

Մարիամ Ասլամազյան Mariam Aslamazyan
Dried peppers. 1983 Mariam M. Aslamazyan

# Two Armenian Summertime Salads

Inspired by the vibrancy of the Aslamazyan sisters' work, these two colourful salads demonstrate how Armenians often pair sweet with savoury and sharpness. Make them for meze-style lunch gatherings or serve as sides for grilled meat and fish.

The slightly unusual second one is an all-time favourite. Take the best red or black grapes you can find, making sure they are seedless, and see how they sing when paired with liquorice-like tarragon, the sweet-sour taste of dried tomatoes and chalky creamy feta.

**BOTH SERVE 4 AS A SIDE**

### CITRUS AND WALNUT SALAD

70g/2½oz walnut halves

1 small orange

1 small firm green apple

2 celery sticks, chopped small, leaves kept

1 tbsp extra-virgin olive oil

1 tbsp lemon juice

Sea salt and freshly ground black pepper, to taste

Begin by toasting the walnuts to bring out their flavour fully. Preheat the oven to 180°C/350°F/gas mark 4. Bake for about 8 minutes, keeping a close eye on them, and remove once they smell roasted. Once cool, break them up to slightly smaller pieces. Peel the orange and remove the pith and seeds carefully. Then, slice it in half and then into crescents. Core the apple (no need to peel it) and cut into thin half-moons. Combine all the salad ingredients with the olive oil and lemon juice and season well.

### GRAPE AND TARRAGON SALAD

1–2 tbsp extra-virgin olive oil, to taste

1 tbsp lemon juice

Sea salt and freshly ground black pepper, to taste

200g/7oz red or black seedless grapes, halved lengthways

80g/2¾oz feta or similar white brined cheese, cubed

Small bunch of tarragon, roughly chopped

50g/1¾oz sundried tomatoes, roughly chopped

Make a dressing first by combining the olive oil and lemon juice with salt and pepper. Carefully combine with the other ingredients, without smooshing the grapes and tarragon too much. Finish with a little more olive oil.

# WE ARE WANDERERS, WE ARE LOST

From Gyumri, we travelled back eastwards to the spa town of Dilijan set on the banks of the Aghstev River, joining horn-blasting weekenders keen to escape Yerevan's ongoing heatwave. All of us were searching for freshness and shade and Dilijan is famous for its national park, leafy with hornbeam, beech and oak. Crucially, it sits at higher altitude, which means temptingly cooler weather.

Feeling journey-tired, we knew that walking would help to shake off travel ennui and would provide an escape from the busy town. Although the clock was already marching towards midday, we quickly identified a walk with a start point just an hour's drive away but remote enough to escape the weekenders. Taking half a day, the circular route, following ancient paths used by herdsmen for generations, promised two highlights: the ruined Bardzrakash Monastery, deep in the Tavut forest, and a 13th-century khachkar called Sirun Khach, which is locally known as the 'beautiful cross stone'. Not only that, a small summertime farmer's market, only in its second year, was scheduled to take place at the starting point in the tiny village of Dsegh. All combined, a good recipe for a classic Armenian walk.

Several things, though, made us hesitate. Firstly, heavy rain was forecast for the whole afternoon. Secondly, it was partly a forest walk. With woodland hiking the views are limited but also, in summer, while the trees provide cover from the sun, they also hold the heat. Recent rainfall meant humidity was guaranteed and the trail would likely be extremely muddy, too. Then there was the late start. With walking the earlier the departure the better; there is more daylight and ample time to drive back. It would be well past lunchtime by the time we actually tied our laces up and set off.

'Come on, let's do it,' said James. 'We can support the market and hopefully get a good lunch, too.'

With waterproofs packed, we jumped into the Lada, which started with the first turn of the key, and off we went slowly snaking through traffic-plugged Dilijan, then climbing upwards past lush green hills and onwards through a thin cooling veil of drizzle. Signposts, suggesting various trails, in English and Armenian, listed threats of reptiles and insects, before adding, in peculiarly military-style language, that walkers ought to be 'physically ready to campaign'. We carried on up to a small mountain plateau, surrounded by misty wildflower meadows. Cars were soon replaced by the odd truck carrying towering hay bales.

The village of Dsegh was quiet but active, the sense of calm made stronger because of the din of Dilijan. Despite it being lunchtime, the farmer's market was just setting up on the village square, tablecloths set onto trestle tables, canopies pegged into grass. We were too early to buy any snacks for our rucksacks but it all felt very well organised.

'Can you sign our visitor's book?' a young girl asked me in perfect English. I said I was going walking but would be back in four or five hours and she said to fill it in anyway, so I did. Suddenly, the day did not seem too late at all. Armenia was reminding us to take things slow, not to rush.

## A POET'S WANDERING HEART

Dsegh was where the great Armenian poet Hovhannes Tumanyan was born, in a hatsatun (bread house), in 1869. At the grand museum dedicated to him in Yerevan sits a small bronze bridal cup he had owned. Its description explained how he'd toast from it when he held feasts at his house. So anticipated were these ceremonies that his friends awarded him the informal title of 'All Armenian Toastmaster'. In the museum bookshop I bought a booklet entitled 'Quatrains' (translated into English by Shushan Avagyan), funded and produced as an act of love by the museum staff themselves, no less, for his 150th anniversary. They even commissioned a new font with the design based on the poet's original manuscripts. Reading the very last inclusion in the book, composed in August 1922, the year before he died, you can easily picture Tumanyan the toastmaster:

'... you are right, so raise your cup!
This too shall pass like a dream, raise your cup!
Life flows through the universe with a zing –

Some live, others wait, raise your cup!'

The famous poem to his daughter, 'A Drop of Honey', based on an Armenian
tale from the Middle Ages, tells how a spilled drop of honey caused bloodshed
between two people who lived in neighbouring villages, and then it grew until
it became a terrible clash amidst different states.

Today, his heart is back home, buried where he was born, in Dsegh. After the
Soviet Union collapsed it was decided by the Minister of Internal Affairs that it
should be returned rather than kept in a glass jar, as it had been, in a museum
belonging to Yerevan's medical university. I wondered if they'd weighed the poet's
heart, like they did with Lenin's brain.

I thought of Tumanyan, and the curious case of his wandering heart, as
we began the walk. Following a thin track first through ploughed fields and
then wilder ones of flowering mallow and chicory and grass as tall and spiky as
porcupine quills, our boots were instantly made heavy by clay-like mud sticky
as treacle. It clung hard and solidly to soles, ruining all grip.

Farms and small cottages with timber cladding ringed the village, some almost
entirely overgrown, just one window or aerial peeking through rampaging
vegetation. All had vegetable plots, fruit trees and hay stacked to the rafters in
sheds. Everywhere, the sound of hens, dogs and cows. Green mountains are here,
too, but they are relatively small, the nearest one, Did, only scaling 1,272 metres.

We saw no other walkers until, entering the forest, we met a small group,
crowded around the freshwater drinking trough of Giqor, which, we learned,
inspired the film *Giqor Mountain Spring*, based on a Tumanyan poem. Each person
took it in turns to drink. The air smelled of gentle rot and mushrooms, vegetal
and soupy, and in the trees goldfinches, Eurasian jays and great tits were busy
chattering. There was much singing from insects, too, vibrating the air. Small
creatures all making their own journeys.

Following a path of slippery ankle-twisting stones laid in the Middle Ages,
the forest grew thicker, and the trail thinner, and we were quickly enveloped
by hornbeam and field maples, cornelian and mahaleb cherry trees. Khachkars,
standing at awkward angles and covered with neon-green lichen, suggested that
we were heading the right way to the ancient monastery, only a few kilometres
from the village.

Then, suddenly, the Bardzrakash Monastery appeared. Dedicated to St Gregory the Illuminator, the first leader of the Armenian Apostolic Church and patron saint of the Armenian people, it was entirely overgrown by vegetation, the forest literally eating it up. With no roof, the first thing you see is a jumble of fallen masonry, memorial stelae scattered around both the 13th-century Mother of God church, and the smaller one to the north side. We wandered among the foundations strewn with priceless cross stones, slabs of perfectly etched medieval Armenian engravings and a new signpost warning that 'it is a sin to write on the walls' though this request had been much ignored. As with many Armenian monasteries, it had been built in the utmost hard to reach place, with the aim of ensuring its sanctuary. The inscriptions hinted at its life story: the earliest one was from the early 1200s, and the last fifty years later. Some suggest the site was abandoned when the Mongols upturned Armenia. I thought of those who first came here, having surrendered their lives for their god, praying for light and glory and knowledge. Closed in prayer, closed again by such solitude and the forest itself. Fed mainly by their faith.

Excavations in the late 1960s have made the ground unsteady and old photographs prove that nothing has been done to save it, apart from the odd clean-up by volunteers, for the past 100 years. I couldn't help but feel dismayed that it was open to looters, graffiti artists and whoever felt they'd like to climb on it. But, I also felt lucky to be there. To simply wander up to this magnificent ruin, without a ticket, without a queue, for it not to be fenced off. I later learned, with some relief, that it is on the watchlist of the World Monuments Fund.

Being there was also a reminder of what happens when dwellings are left to nature. As a quiet, peaceful place left alone, it has become, if not a remote altar for people today, then a place where at least plant and animal life thrives. Beetles scuttled through nooks lacy with cobwebs, birds sang from the exposed arches. No doubt larger animals emerged at night.

Forests are important to the Armenian people as can be seen not only by religious sites scattered throughout the landscape but also picnic areas in the most remote spots. But there is a decrease in forest cover, first from the period of industrial growth of the 1930s, then from wood harvested for heating and cooking. Oak forests are being killed off by caterpillars and brown-tail moths which kill the young trees.

### GATA AND WHITE FIGS

We walked on, for an hour or so, first using a cattle driving route for direction, fresh cow pats showing the way, then a water pipe that led to a village far below, but quickly the woods became thicker, and, pushing branches to the side as we

went, soon enough we were not able to see very far in any direction. All markers had disappeared.

Every walk has its own unique set of risks and at this stage, the hazard was silent and unseen. But it was there. When the undergrowth did thin out, I looked to my left and gasped. A ravine, two hundred metres or so to a river below, and the edge perilously close. You'd be unlucky to fall, but just one stumble could be fatal.

We carried on carefully and a bit later met three unaccompanied donkeys on the path. Then other, weirder, things began to appear. Plastic water bottles hanging from branches, and a bit further on, a rough rifle stand made from wood. Then, just by it, beside the ripped-out back seat of a car, a sort of bed. A hunter's den. The atmosphere became eerie.

We moved on again, a little quicker, which was perhaps a mistake because after just a couple of kilometres, the second threat presented itself. A dreadful sense of the woods crowding in and the bitter realisation that we were lost. The route a map shows is only good if it is maintained.

The trail was so badly overgrown, so impossibly thick with oppressive vegetation and obstacles, fallen trees and thick spiky bushes, that walking had become not only taxing but impossible. Even though I knew we were not far from villages, I suddenly felt giddily remote. Branches kept catching my damp hair and face and every time I stopped to clear the way with my trekking pole, grievous mosquitoes landed on me and ants inched up my legs, while never-ending tiny black flies hovered maddeningly right in front of my eyeballs and crawled into my ears. I was becoming a source, prey, and so a small psychological battle began.

In very thick woodland everything looks the same and walking in a straight line becomes almost unworkable. Without any landmarks to navigate with, you inevitably start looping about. The feeling of being off-course, the realisation of it, is always a shock no matter how many times you have been disorientated before. Raised, as we are, on folklore and horror movies, being lost in the woods, where there might be wolves, axe-wielding maniacs, bands of outlaws, giants or Baba Yaga, produces a primeval visceral feeling. As James was turning this way and that with the compass, I pictured robbers springing from the shadows.

Nowadays, in our smartphone age, it is easy to think it is impossible to get lost, that GPS will find the way, but sat nav often fails. All experienced walkers know that when one thing goes wrong the situation can quickly spiral downhill: you get lost, the weather worsens, you get cold, your phone battery dies, blazes painted on trees suddenly disappear, forests have sprung up since your map was produced making it useless, rain dissolves your map, you get hungry or thirsty, and you end up missing, swallowed by the forest. The key rule is to pay attention, to remember which way you came in so that you can always turn back. There is no fear akin to feeling truly lost. Fear befogs any problem solving, logical thoughts of direction, time, how far you walked and from which direction are all upset. Feeling lost can feel like claustrophobia mixed with an impending panic attack.

We backtracked a little and eventually walked out into open fields. My battle with the bugs, and my fears, lessened. I came back to my body, aware again of my breathing, mindful of each step, of lungs, heart, legs, no longer concerned with losing the way. But still that specific forest feeling lingered on: a feeling of being watched.

As we carried on, the walk became liquid once more, flowing again, and I wondered about the stones used to build the monastery, how they were transported, and at what cost of labour. And I thought of my guidebook which had mentioned the larger birds of the surrounding gorge, specifically lammergeiers, Europe's largest vultures, also known (in colonial language) as 'vultures of the old world'.

Slowly, the forest-edged fields turned into open countryside which we strode across until we reached the lonely Sirun Khach, a favourite monument of poet Tumanyan, according to the signpost. Glistening in the damp, it had been sculpted from light brown tuff and reverently set on a triple-stepped pedestal of black basalt. This moment called for a hill snack reward so I pulled out a packet of gozinaki, a sweet brittle made of nuts and seeds, and we snapped pieces off.

Not wanting to miss the farmer's market, we tramped on through a beautiful meadow, with foals and wild oregano and cornflowers, until we reached the small country houses surrounding the village, and finally the solid ground of the market area.

Lingering over the well-stocked stalls we bought what we should have taken with us for a picnic: hot revitalising coffee, gata, a litre of fresh pumpkin juice, a cheese turnover, lavash dotted with sesame seeds and a kilo of exceptional white figs bought from the boot of a car belonging to the woman who'd picked them from her garden. There was some amiable rivalry between the stallholders for who had the biggest and best, rarest and freshest raspberries and we bought two cups from different vendors to taste the difference.

Armenia's bumper harvest was as round and promising as the gata I held in my hand: in summer its produce is fresh, in winter it is pickled. A never-ending cycle. Exhausted, we collapsed into the car with our haul.

# Gozinaki – Snack Bars

An excellent energy-filled treat that is perfect for stuffing into a jacket pocket ahead of a walk. Usually, gozinaki is made with half honey, half walnuts, while this version offers a slightly wider variation and is a little less sugary. In the Georgia section of this book is a recipe which sees it go into cinnamon ice cream, a good way to use up any excess or spare bars (page 172).

**MAKES 12 BARS**

300g/10½oz mixed nuts (I used hazelnuts, cashews, blanched almonds and walnuts)

1 tbsp sesame seeds

125g/4½oz honey

40g/1½oz brown sugar

Line a baking sheet with very lightly oiled parchment paper. Toast the nuts and sesame seeds in a dry frying pan then transfer to a food processor and pulse to a very coarse rubble.

Next, place a deep saucepan over a low heat and slowly warm the honey and sugar until liquid. Stir in the nuts and seeds until thickened and coming together, you can add a little more honey if needed, and to taste, but I think this is better not too sweet.

Once cool enough to handle, spread the mixture in a thick layer, about 15cm/6in square, on the lined baking sheet. Put in the refrigerator for 20 minutes or so until firm and, when ready, slide the gozinaki, still on the paper, onto a chopping board and cut into bars to keep in an airtight container.

# Chicken with White Wine and Walnut Sauce

At a restaurant in Dilijan we ate roast chicken that had, to me, a distinctly Georgian flavour given the wine and walnut sauce. To serve with it, I suggest keeping it simple with a green salad, a plate of sliced tomatoes or a cucumber and herb salad.

**SERVES 4**

1 whole free-range chicken without giblets (about 1.5kg/3lb 5oz)

Juice of ½ lemon

1 tbsp olive oil

1½ tsp sea salt flakes

Freshly ground black pepper

½ tsp sweet paprika

½ tsp red pepper flakes

**FOR THE SAUCE**

60g/2¼oz walnuts

1 large garlic clove, roughly chopped

½ tsp ground coriander

¼ tsp ground blue fenugreek

½ tsp ground cumin

Juice of ½ lemon

100ml/scant ½ cup hot chicken stock

2 tbsp white wine

Sea salt and freshly ground black pepper

Preheat the oven to 200°C/400°F/gas mark 6. Remove any fat around the cavity of the chicken. Squeeze over the lemon juice, drizzle with the oil, season the chicken inside and out and sprinkle over the spices. Put the squeezed lemon half into the cavity. Place in a roasting tin, breast side down, and roast the chicken for 1 hour, or until the juices run clear after piercing the thigh and there is no pink meat. Cover and leave in a warm place to rest while you make the sauce.

Toast the walnuts in a small, dry frying pan then put all the ingredients, except the stock and wine, in a food processor and whizz until you have a wet sand texture. Transfer it to a saucepan and add the hot stock and any juices from the resting chicken. Simmer for 10 minutes, stirring often until thickened, then add the wine, and cook down again for a couple of minutes until you have a hummus-like sauce. Remove from the heat, leave to cool to room temperature and check the seasoning.

Serve the chicken hot or cold with the walnut sauce.

# LUNCH WITH THE MILK DRINKERS

Walking through the village of Lermontovo, some 20 kilometres west of Dilijan and named after the Moscow-born writer Mikhail Lermontov, author of *A Hero of Our Time: Sketches of Russian Life in the Caucasus* (1840), we were met with a scene that looked how I imagined an Amish village might look if you moved it from Ohio to the South Caucasus. Girls, keeping their hair covered by headscarves, wore white blouses, long skirts in flowery prints or pinafore dresses, while the boys, dressed in trousers and shirts, looked painfully shy. When we tried to talk to people, most shook their heads, looked down, and walked away. Heavy clouds hung in the surrounding hills casting shadows on the parquetry of valleys making the small village feel entirely cut off.

A group of men in their twenties, visiting their grandparents who were born here, agreed to talk to us. They explained that their community is spread across three villages, that their name 'milk drinkers' or Molokans, was a nickname given to them by the Orthodox church, which their ancestors had broken away from. Across the border in Azerbaijan there is just one Molokan village left, Ivanovka. Pork isn't eaten, they explained, and a mixture of the Old and New Testament is followed. Fires are not lit on the rest day, which for them is Sunday, not Saturday. And because it is Sunday, the day we'd turned up, there is no work, no lighting of fires to cook, much like in Orthodox Judaism. And it's not a church they gather at on holy days, they went on to tell us, but someone's home. There are no idols either. 'Church is the people, not the structure or building, we follow that rule,' one man said.

Two older women, Tatiana and Katerina, stopped to say hello. They told us that while they have Armenian neighbours this village is 80 per cent Russian. They are grandmothers now and have lived in the village their whole lives where they like to grow apples and pumpkins but not apricots as it's too cold. When they saw the camera in my hand, they politely said: 'No photographs, thank you.' They, like all the villagers, obey a long-held refusal when it comes to having their picture taken by outsiders.

We carried on walking, past fields and fields of cabbages and neat A-frame houses tucked behind steel gates decorated with swans, grapes or daisies. The village gardens were in full bloom with yellow lilies, poppies and roses. Ducks waddled in pairs down the main dirt street.

Piotr, with a bushy beard and a flat cap, and one gold tooth at the front, stopped to talk next, asking us where we were from. When I returned the question, he replied 'Here, but we are Russian first, then Molokan.' Young people go to the city to work, older people stay here and grow food, he said before leaving us with a smile.

We asked around whether there was a café or a guesthouse, somewhere we could find out more. 'Natalya and Mikhail's place in the next village,' we were told by a young man wanting to practise his English. 'It's not a café but you can go there. A few kilometres that way,' he said pointing.

## SUNFLOWERS AND SAMOVARS

Natalya and Mikhail Rudometkin's house isn't signposted but they welcome the few travellers who drift in. They have even had a business card made, with the words 'relax in the village of Fioletovo', in Russian, printed on it, alongside a drawing of an 130-year-old samovar they own, a symbol of hospitality. We visited before the full-scale invasion of Ukraine but as I write this, I cannot help wishing I had the chance to ask them what they think about Putin's appalling warmongering.

'Come in, come in,' Natalya said. We stepped into a courtyard where chickens clucked and giant sunflowers had been painted on the walls. In lieu of a refrigerator, cold water ran continually over jugs of milk in a bucket to keep it fresh.

'This is where we have hosted foreigners, French, Italians, Americans, in the summertime for the past seven years. They come here to rest. Today we cannot work, or cook, so please come back tomorrow? Or whenever you like, just ring the day before and say hello.' Natalya went on, explaining how the food they would eat today was made on Saturday, yesterday, because they are not allowed to work on a Sunday. Six days to work, one to relax.

'A while ago someone came here and made a book about our village.' I ask whether we can buy it but then we realise it is Sunday. No work, no sales!

'Everyone makes mistakes,' Natalya laughed good naturedly.

'When the Soviet Union fell we had to go back to simple farming because there was a lack of trucks and petrol,' Mikhail said, flicking through the book.

In the main dining room, where we chatted, four more giant samovars gleamed on the windowsill. Beyond, was the garden, ridiculously verdant with cabbages, carrots and potatoes, a burbling stream, mineral water spring and a river a little further away for fishing.

The next day, we returned, and were ushered inside to join Mikhail who was wearing everyday clothes unlike yesterday when he was in his best: a white collarless linen shirt as traditionally worn in Russian villages and sash belt. Baron, their dog, was out in the yard with the cows.

As we sat down to eat, Mikhail told us more about their lives. 'We speak Russian but we are Armenian citizens, we have an Armenian passport. The villagers all do Armenian conscription but we don't have much contact day to day. Sometimes we need an Armenian translator for things,' he said, before Natalya chimed in to add matter-of-factly, 'We cannot really be Armenians because we are Russians.'

Lunch was served and Natalya slapped back and forth across the floor in slippers with bowls of food. She brought rich buttery homemade lapsha (noodles in a thick broth), served with a special lacquered Khokhloma-style spoon; a peach salad with cucumbers, tomato and garden herbs; a plate of warm potato and cabbage pirozhki (small pies that look more like buns); another of whole chestnut mushrooms filled with strong garlic and herbs; cabbage and carrot slaw. Mountain water. Rye bread. Homemade cheese. Wild raspberry jam, pear and apricot jam. Meanwhile, Mikhail's job was to keep pouring from the old samovar.

Natalya explained that she can't get rye flour for bread here, so her son brings it from Moscow, and that he still keeps a house in the village. As we eat we are shown photographs of their family, colour images of Victory Day and weddings, of three children – two sons and a daughter – and eight grandchildren. 'All went to Russia in the 1990s when life was hard here, mainly to Krasnodar, not far from the Black Sea.'

We all ate the warm pirozhki, and I said, in truth, 'These are the best pirozhki I ever ate.'

'I know!' answered Natalya with a giggle.

Finally, garlicky kholodets (jellied meat) was brought out, made from beef. It was put on white bread as a health-giving snack.

'Try it,' said Natalya. 'Only if you want to,' added Mikhail with a grin. Kholodets is an acquired taste. As we eat, Natalya talks about how she loves

Georgia with its strong sun, good fruit and wine. And how hard the winters are in the village of Fioletovo when the streets turn into tunnels of snow.

We ask about their daily routine and are told that at six in the morning a shepherd takes their cows up into the hills, then they return a couple of hours later.

'Of course we name the cows. They are Zoyka, Ramashka and Lenka. They are like pets, we call out to them, and they come.' And Natalya admits she is a rare Russian babushka who isn't a cat person. 'Cats are for cities.'

Nowadays, the couple have become the face of the village. Nobody else wants to take curious outsiders, who generally turn up to see how a traditional Molokan village operates in Armenia, into their homes, and there is a wariness. People want to keep the village 'as is' and do not welcome change.

During the Soviet era, Azerbaijanis would come during the hot summer and many would host them. But things are, of course, different now. It took a savvy tour operator from Yerevan, who came and was fascinated but had nowhere to stay, who encouraged the Rudometkins to open their doors and to make use of their large space. At the start, their openness to visitors did initially cause some tensions, with neighbours staring from their windows, 'spying', Natalya said, making a binoculars sign with her hands, before adding, 'you do need some patience to do this.' And a lot of charm, which Natalya and Mikhail have plenty of. One day, she continued, two groups in huge tour buses came, a hundred people or so, tourists from Germany. 'They came to see us! It was fine as we like to have visitors. And it was simple really, I just cooked an enormous pot of borscht and fed them all.'

As we set to leave, the village seemed to offer a parting message to us as well. That while Armenia's identity and national spirit is strong, it is also more varied than it may at first appear.

# Peach Salad with Garden Greens

Usually, peaches are grilled when added to salad but Natalya Rudometkin, trusting the quality of those grown in her garden in Fioletovo, just chops the fruit and adds the slices into her savoury salads. I liked this style but it does require the very best peaches you can find.

**SERVES 4 AS A SIDE**

4 peaches, stoned and sliced

100g/3½oz lamb's lettuce (mâche)

1 small cucumber, diced

2 large tomatoes, diced

Handful of dill and parsley, chopped

**FOR THE DRESSING**

3 tbsp extra-virgin olive oil

1 tbsp sherry vinegar

Sea salt and freshly ground black pepper

If the ingredients are good they need little interference, just gently mix, and dress.

# Potato and Cabbage Pirozhki for Natalya and Mikhail Rudometkin

These little 'hand pies', inspired by the ones served by Natalya Rudometkin in the Molokan village of Fioletovo, are as good for the picnic basket as they are for the lunch table, transportable and moreish as they are. I like to have a small bowl of ketchup or mayonnaise ready for dipping them into, though they are tasty on their own.

**MAKES 16**

### FOR THE DOUGH

250g/1¾ cups plain (all-purpose) flour, plus extra for dusting

7g/¼oz fast-action dried yeast

½ tsp fine sea salt

½ tsp caster (superfine) sugar

115ml/scant ½ cup whole milk

1 egg

1 tbsp sunflower oil

### FOR THE FILLING

1 tbsp sunflower oil, plus extra to finish

1 tsp caraway seeds

1 onion, grated

1 carrot, grated

1 large potato, boiled and mashed

170g/6oz sauerkraut, drained

Small handful of finely chopped dill

Small handful of finely chopped parsley

Sea salt flakes and freshly ground black pepper

For the dough, put the flour into a large mixing bowl, then add the yeast to one side, the salt and sugar to the other. Whisk together the milk, egg and sunflower oil in a jug, then make a well in the flour and pour in. Mix until you have a shaggy dough. Turn out the dough onto a lightly floured surface and knead until the stickiness has gone, 10 minutes or so. Place in a lightly oiled bowl, cover with a damp tea towel and leave to rise in a warm spot for at least an hour, or until doubled in size.

Meanwhile, make the filling. Warm the oil in a large frying pan, add the caraway seeds and fry until their scent is released. Add a generous pinch each of salt and pepper, along with the onion and carrot, and sauté for 5 minutes. Remove from the heat and allow to cool.

In a large bowl, combine the potato, sauerkraut and herbs, then add the cooled sautéed vegetables, adding more salt and pepper. Combine the filling well.

Line 2 baking trays with baking parchment.

Cut the risen dough into quarters. Working with one quarter at a time (keep the dough you are not immediately using covered with the damp tea towel, to stop it drying out), divide the piece into four again. Lightly flour the surface, then roll each quarter into a 10cm/4in round. Add roughly 2 tablespoons of the filling to the centre of each round, then bring up the sides of the dough to enclose the filling, pinching and pleating along the top to seal. Repeat with the remaining dough. Once all 16 pies are assembled, place them on the lined trays, seam-side down, then let them rise again for 20 minutes in a warm place.

Meanwhile, preheat the oven to 200°C/400°F/gas mark 6.

Pinch closed any splits in the risen pies, then brush with oil and bake for 20–30 minutes, or until golden. Serve at room temperature. They'll keep in an airtight container for a couple of days and can be gently reheated in the oven.

# PART TWO

# GEORGIA

# A ONE-MILE RADIUS TO TASTE TBILISI

Tbilisi is a patchwork city, of the recently arrived and the long established, where new houses rise from the rubble of the old and oranges and lemons are sold under wrought-iron balconies, latticed musharabi screens, porthole windows and Art Nouveau facades. In the shadow of grey basalt Stalinist-era apartments, pocket-sized bakeries sell gondola-shaped bread and glazed wooden courtyards are criss-crossed with laundry lines. A map is misleading because it tells you none of these things. It is only by putting in a little time, on foot, that you come to know such fragments of Tbilisi.

A year on from Russia's full-scale invasion of Ukraine, I arrived from Istanbul with a plan to stay a while, catching up with an assortment of friends who for various reasons – love, money, music, business, journalism – have made the Georgian capital home. It was February and everyone says February is a bad month to be in Tbilisi, but that isn't true. A bright sky, more often than not, follows a bleak sky. No, the worst time to be in Tbilisi is the height of summer when the temperature is unbearable and the streets are crowded, both of which make walking miserable.

Tbilisi had changed since I first visited, in 2013. Public spaces had been spruced, the variety of hotels, cafés, bars and restaurants (craft ale! bagels!) was far greater and everyone nowadays uses taxi apps to get around rather than waving down a random car on the street driven by someone who may, or may not, be moonlighting to make some extra cash. Everything seemed faster, and, accordingly, prices had risen. It was hard to remember exactly what it had been like in 2013 – my earliest impressions had been blurred by visiting a couple of times since – but occasionally, by turning a certain corner off the main avenue Rustaveli, or by sucking in a particular smell in the underpasses, feelings that had laid hidden somewhere resurfaced: how back then I'd felt a bigger feeling of distance from home; how back then, there was more of a sense of slow motion. In 2013, James and I had stayed with a legendary woman named Manana who offered rooms and dinner by word-of-mouth. Places to stay were quite limited and it was an arrangement that proved intimate and interesting. We had the top floor of her classic old Tbilisi townhouse, not far from the opera, complete with a jacuzzi bath, and every evening when we went out, after we'd shared some family wine, she'd yell behind us in English, 'Don't do drugs!', a government-sounding slogan she'd picked up somewhere. I was never entirely sure if she was joking or not.

On this latest visit, the challenge, I quickly found out, was not the weather, though it was snowy, smoggy and cold, it was finding somewhere to stay. As I'd been warned, hardly anything was available because self-imposed Russian exiles had snapped up everything half-decent while pushing skywards the cost of all short-term lets (decent or not).

Eventually, I found a place. The flat was a twenty-minute walk from Marjanishvili Metro station down David Agmashenebeli Avenue, named after King David Agmashenebeli, aka David the Builder, who reigned from 1089 to 1125, in the Chugureti district, close to the Constructivist-style citadel complex of the Tumanishvili Theatre of Film Actors and the former German embassy. A piece of graffitied Berlin Wall remains today, marooned in the courtyard.

Located on the top floor, by the front door a sticker declared 'Putin get out!', and a shashlik grill stood with a cover neatly over it, retired for winter. Inside the three-room apartment (bedroom, bathroom, living area/kitchen) were views out towards the awnings of the Dezerter's Bazaar, which got its name from soldiers who, over a hundred years ago, allegedly sold their kit at the market.

As I moved in temporarily, David Agmashenebeli Avenue, ringed by theatres, went about its business: dogs barked, children yelled at a performance clown, people slipped over on ice and from behind locked doors families argued. Slowly, the district crept up on me. I'd set myself a goal to try and learn what I could in a one-mile radius around the flat. It had more than enough. As well as being theatreland, it was close to the famous bazaar, and there was Barbarestan, one of Georgia's most celebrated and established restaurants. This is where, if you show interest, the waiter comes to your table with an old wooden box, which he will open ceremoniously with a key to present to you a glimpse of a very old cookbook by Duchess Barbare Eristavi Jorjadze, which inspires the restaurant's menu. And on the table you'll find not one set, but two sets of salt and pepper shakers (why share?) and your soup broth might be poured straight from a teapot at the table (as mine was). In that sense, it is both touristy but quintessentially, and eccentrically, Tbilisian. There is no doubt that while Barbarestan has been overtaken by newer, trendier dining spots (reviewers are fickle and competitive), it still manages to hold onto more than a little magic.

Continuing cold and dry, the weather forecast threatened frost and snow flurries. Such weather required the right shoes, gloves and hat but there was no reason to sit indoors and so I booked a walking tour through the Dezerter's Bazaar with my friend, the journalist Paul Rimple, an expat of two decades, who has an infectious ease and a good appetite for the best amusements of life: wine, humour, food, writing and music.

'I have a shopping list,' said Paul as we began walking, under a hard blue sky, into the market's chatty jumble, the sounds of conspiratorial mutterings surrounding us, as if everyone was gossiping or plotting something. If you don't know, it can be hard to figure out where the market begins, where the centre is, or even where to enter.

In about 2006 some of the old buildings were knocked down in order to clean things up, to have everyone off the street. 'Inside, the old bazaar building, the one with red brick, you get an idea of how it used to be, all intense, all enclosed, the butchers, the cheese ladies and the spice ladies, and little chacha [pomace] stands, I'd come with my friend Zaza, and he'd sing his song, "The Apple Seller",' Paul said, beginning to reminisce.

As we ate warm lobiani, bean-filled bread, bought from a hole-in-the-wall baker, we discussed the evolution of markets and produce and how they reflect changing tastes. 'Lettuce was hard to find years ago, but then one restaurant started selling Caesar salad, and so the others had to put it on their menu too, and it grew like that,' Paul said. I later read that lettuce may have originated in the Caucasus, as long as six thousand years ago.

We walked on, past pyramids of nubbly golden quince and huge plastic tubs of peeled garlic cloves shining like shark's teeth, but the market constantly distracted us, forcing us to stop, with its colours and textures. In front of a display of tiny spring onions, next to dried plums and radishes, we nibbled a little sprig of purslane, fresh and minty tasting, and suddenly Paul was surrounded by the lemon ladies. He knows them all – they are selling fruit from the Samegrelo region where the superlative Meyer lemon variety has been grown since the last century. One roaming vendor with red nails and fingerless gloves has, alongside her lemons, shiny green chillies in a green plastic basket. The sun, emboldening the colours, made the scene appear like a still-life painting. He buys from her, saying to the other lemon ladies, 'shemdeg, shemdeg', which means after, or in this context, next time. Competition for even a small sale is fierce. 'They're good about it, but the cheese ladies are a bit more feisty.'

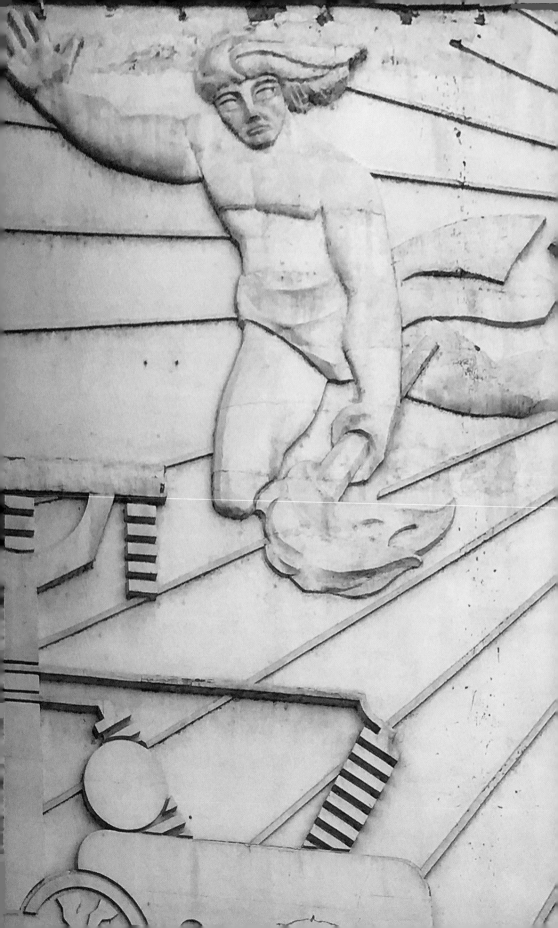

We carried on, putting a little distance between us and the citrus sellers, going past a clutter of market cats sunning themselves under a display of leathery pomegranates and displays of candlestick-like churchela, sweetmeats of walnuts, threaded together and dipped in grape molasses, of varying quality. Some are mass-produced and far too hard on the teeth but we agreed that they are a fine travel snack ('when you're marching off to war, churchela!', Paul half-joked). I thought of the neon-coloured churchela sold at Privoz market, in Odesa, across the Black Sea, and I wondered how the vendor I'd photographed there was faring today.

Entering a hall, we were met by a strong smell of creamy milk mixed with pickles marinating in tubs. A small scrappy dog, being steered along on a market trolley, stared at us with suspicion before barking ferociously. 'This area is liveliest during apple season but now it's the end of that season,' Paul said, trying, but failing, to calm the dog down. Most of the produce here in winter has come from western Georgia or in big containers from Turkey. In summertime, hundreds of minivans arrive here from all over the country with local, seasonal produce.

A piece of walnut membrane is slid from Paul's hand to mine. It is used to flavour chacha, a grappa-like drink made from fermented grape skins and seeds left over from winemaking, and is also put into tea for an immunity boost. Chacha, known as mountain fire, is unnervingly strong and Georgians love it. The walnuts have come from Kakheti, east of Tbilisi, and Paul demonstrates the best way to test their quality, by gently digging a nail into the flesh. The more oil that seeps out, the better. Another superlative thing to eat in Georgia, we agree, is yogurty matsoni, thick and tangy, especially when paired with sweet syrupy walnut preserve. 'Start the day with matsoni!', we chimed. In wintertime, when cows aren't eating a lot of grass, supermarket matsoni tends to be made from powdered milk but out in the countryside, in warm weather, it is very special.

We moved on. Past tkemali (plum sauce) stalls, piles of feijoa, a fruit native to South America but also grown in Georgia to be used for chacha or kompot. Many people sell similar produce but each vendor has one particular way of doing things and each stall is individualised: an icon here, a garland there. As with all markets, public property mixes freely with the deeply personal.

Upstairs, where vendors were hatted with hoods and beanies to keep off the cold, we became further absorbed by the market. Stopping by one cheese stand with an impressive display of springy sourish Imeretian cheese, chalk-white sulguni, rounds of 'factory cheese' (a little like cheddar) and strips of smoked sulguni, which instantly reminded me of twisty strings of braided chechil (the bar snack popular in Central Asia and Russia). Given their soft surfaces, many whole cheeses had been branded by the weave of the basket in which they'd been set, giving them chequered patterns. Everyone was chatting, and sharing their advice. 'You should never buy cheese from sellers with dirty fingernails,' advised one cheesemonger. Another told us that his ideal lunch would be guda, aged in sheepskin, from northeastern Georgia, served with wine and a salad of fresh tarragon. I tried the guda from a knife blade he proffered – it was very salty but the aftertaste quickly mellowed. Another vendor, one of Paul's neighbours (this is a market of relationships formed over years), insisted we try his nadugi: thin sulguni rolled around curd, soft and creamy. As I ate it, enraptured, he said to Paul that tourists in the market now tend to be Russian or Belarussian. He nodded at me before asking, 'You, America?'

Next to the cheese sellers, cacti grew out of yogurt tubs and light shone through stained glass. Pinned to the walls were calendars from yesteryear still kept, presumably, for their glossy images of Mount Kazbek, tigers, babies and kittens. And there was a little market shrine in one corner, an icon station with oil lamps and pictures of the Virgin Mary and Jesus. Vintage weighing scales, painted baby blue, older than me. We weaved through a room of several suckling pig counters – grimly medical-looking with blood stains, refrigerators, butchering tables and scattered knives – all repeated in tilted reflective glass attached to the ceiling, like a gruesome hall of mirrors.

'On New Year's Eve everyone eats suckling pig. Some bakers roast a pig in their oven, best if it is a wood burner, though there are less of those nowadays,' Paul said. As I paid for a bottle of pomegranate juice, another wandering saleswoman sensed an opportunity and came up behind me, purring: 'Svaneti salt, put on salad and … ooooffff!' She held a bag of it right under my nose so that I'd get the idea. 'Where are you?' another woman yelled at me above a pyramid of cornflour (really asking where I was from). I laughed, answered, and then she shouted back 'I, Georgia!'

'Pleased to meet you,' said a halal butcher from Azerbaijan, appropriately named Aliyev, like the country's president. Surrounded by bloody ribs, Paul leaned in to tell me that Aliyev may be Muslim, and only sells halal meat, and strictly no pork, but he means business with his chacha. 'Do you want a shot? This one, you don't want to sip, though,' Paul whispered, putting a piece of dried persimmon in my palm to be eaten as the chaser. Aliyev handed me a paper coffee cup brimming with innocently clear chacha. 'Only one, it's pretty early,' I said, thanking him. I knocked it back as the sound of cleavers coming down into hunks of meat reverberated around the hall.

'To health!' says Aliyev. 'Holy shit,' I gasped, shaking my head. It was brain-damagingly strong. As my throat cooled slightly, my nostrils flared. The butchers all clapped. Someone put a cashew in my hand, which I ate gratefully.

We continued. Caviar from Russia. Norwegian salmon. Sturgeon from Kazakhstan. And with that I'm again transported back to Tbilisi in 2013, when Manana, our host, would yell 'shashlik!' up the stairs when dinner was ready and James and I would join her in the kitchen to have a meal of Georgian wine with fatty sturgeon shashlik. 'Ah, sturgeon, you used to get it on all the restaurant menus, it was one of the most expensive things to order, but no more,' said Paul. A reminder again of changing tastes.

There was only a little fish for sale from the Black Sea. Sensing my interest, Paul dived into the subject, suggesting that the fishing trade took a bad turn in the 1990s, when Georgia's fishing rights were sold to Ukraine and Turkey. Back then, the fishing industry was in disrepair, nobody was investing in it, and largely, that is still the case today. These rules, signed years ago, are hard to turn around and anyway, Georgians are not big fish eaters. Catfish in vinegar appears on menus, though every time I tried to order it in Tbilisi it wasn't available. Later, outside, we found some dorado from the Black Sea on sale, a kitten eyeing it keenly. The fish counters were mostly in a sorry state, with large fish crammed into tanks. In one, a dead fish floated upside down, its fin sticking out of the water, a symbol perhaps of the neglected business. It could not be more different, across the Black Sea, in Turkey where fish is revered.

From the apartment, I continued wandering the one-mile radius that I'd set myself, buffeted against the cold in layers of clothes and always careful not to slip over on the slush. At number 189 David Agmashenebeli Avenue is the Tramworkers' Houses building, which according to my architectural guidebook was the first Soviet housing complex in Tbilisi, 'eight three-storey buildings arranged around a central courtyard'. Built in 1926, and designed to house 1,500 residents in 126 units, it encompassed 'shared amenities that would elevate the socialist labourer: a clinic, laundry, dining hall, bathhouse, and library.'

Then, there is the Maria Stern House, at number 149, one of the most eye-catching buildings on the whole street, a palace set back from the traffic and with a fountain at the front by thin Cypress trees. It is magnificent, though when I asked around, nobody seemed to know what it was built for, or why. I referred to the guidebook again which told me it belonged to the German architect, Paul Stern (active between 1870–1915), architect of the Tbilisi Art Palace and overseer of the Moorish-style opera house. In the early 19th century, Russian colonisation incentives brought Germans to the Caucasus. Many lived right here, excelling not only at architecture but in growing fruit trees, beer-brewing and winemaking. Tbilisi City Hall and the National Gallery are also the work of German-Georgians. Today, this history lives on and David Agmashenebeli Avenue, with its Turkish restaurants and barbers and small offices belonging to dentists and lawyers, felt unique, slightly removed from the more intensely touristy parts of town.

Most days, I'd buy fresh bread, too hot to touch and therefore handed over wrapped in a piece of graph paper, on the impossible-to-say Mikheil Tsinamdzgvrishvili Street. The baker was often out of sight, but could be heard singing somewhere near the clay oven, so the face of the enterprise was a woman who had a habit of dressing entirely in red – nails, jacket, little padded replica Chanel handbag – and she'd take the money. Sometimes, I'd carry my bread, nibbling on the heel of it (it is impossible not to do this) while wandering towards the city centre past the Khrushchev-era concrete mass housing and traditional buildings that had been 'restroyed' (restored but destroyed in the process). Past old houses with their tenuous street-facing latticed balconies and courtyards with dozens of wooden-framed windows, and onwards through underpasses with their poetic graffiti: 'he whose face gives no light shall be no star', as spotted on Mtatsminda Street, and 'only lovers left alive' (likely a reference to the Jim Jarmusch film, a movie Tbilisian in its melancholic leanings), as seen on Giga Lortkipanidze Street. Invariably, I'd treat myself to an experimental ice cream at The Cone Culture kiosk on Taras Shevchenko Street (named for the hero–poet of Ukraine), usually gozinaki (nuts caramelised in honey; see page 139) and cinnamon, a flavour for all seasons.

Or I'd have lunch, white tablecloths and all, at the Vinotel, on a hill named after the artist Elene Akhvlediani who painted Tbilisi so colourfully in the 20th century, mainly as I loved the garden and the rug-filled anteroom and the coriander soup which would be poured at the table into bowls directly from a saucière. At the other end of things, I'd have a cup of tea at Sabir's Chaikhana, a cellar tea house introduced to me by Paul Rimple and located in the ancient bath district of Abanotubani, filled with men smoking cigarettes. Run by a former manager of one of the ancient bathhouses, it reminded me of chaikhanas in Central Asia. Legend has it that in the 5th century, king Vakhtang I of Iberia happened upon hot sulphur springs while hunting a pheasant (or a deer; nobody can agree), he wounded the creature and it ran to the sulphur spring and emerged immediately healed from the hot waters (just like the Armenian legend in the spa town of Jermuk), though others suggest it was instantly cooked. With that, he decided to establish a city on the spot.

As the days passed, eventually I found myself looking for a reason to leave the city and to my surprise one afternoon, I got one. My phone lit up with a string of messages: 'I'm heading up to Mestia for Lamproba, it's on Valentine's Day but it happens at night. It is very snowy and trekking is difficult, but I know a good driver. Come, it'll be fun.' My friend, Amelia Stewart, who lives in Tbilisi and leads tours throughout Georgia, and elsewhere in the world, had sent the messages. I Googled Lamproba (and found out that it is a gathering with pagan origins that takes place at different graveyards in Svaneti when families light birch branches to warm the souls of the dead) and wondered if it was madness to drive all the way up into Upper Svaneti, where the little town of Mestia sits, in winter. We all know that saints stuck on dashboards aren't enough to protect you on mountain roads, especially in bad weather.

I took my feelings of uncertainty to a basement restaurant, named Ghebi, close to my rented flat, a sort of joyously anonymous place where you can be whoever you want and nobody bothers you. There, I fed the wall-mounted jukebox, one lari a song, so that I could hear Edith Piaf and Charles Aznavour. I drank beer, and ate mushroom khinkali, the broth deeply savoury and steaming. Everyone eats these dumplings in the same way: you marvel at their simple bulbous perfection, like flat-bottomed white onions, when they arrive, magnificent on the plate, and then lament them when they are gone, all too quickly, the nubs remaining as evidence on the plate (it is a culinary outrage to eat those).

At Ghebi, Georgian families and groups of young Russians all ate similarly affordable meals, served to them by friendly waiting staff dressed in navy and white uniforms with name badges affixed to their chests. And as in most cafés and restaurants in Tbilisi, everyone appeared to rub along just fine.

But visa-free travel and direct flights between Russia and Georgia, while much of Europe had banned both, was driving a lot of anger against the Georgian government. Many Georgians strongly support Ukraine while resenting Moscow for its long history of tormenting and dismembering their nation. Many also actively want stronger ties to the EU. But others have greatly benefited financially from Russians who, fleeing conscription and a country which had become increasingly strangulating, kept arriving, kept renting apartments and kept registering businesses in Georgia. The graffiti all over town, often making use of the 'Z' symbol, the one Putin's troops decorated their tanks with, highlighted the distaste and fear: 'Ruzz are occupiers', 'Ruzzia is a terrorist state' and 'Ruzzki not welcome'. There was a palpable buzz of tension. I messaged my friend Amelia, saying I'd join her. Tbilisi had begun to close in a bit.

# Red Tkemali – Sour Plum Sauce

As I discovered, tkemali is extremely versatile, going well alongside roasted new potatoes as well as baked salmon fillets, or with Sunday roasts and barbecued meat.

**MAKES 1 LARGE JAR**

1 tsp caraway seeds

1 tsp dill seeds

½ tsp coriander seeds

600g/1lb 5oz red plums (about 7 fruits)

1 garlic clove, roughly chopped

Scant ¼ tsp fine sea salt

¼ tsp cayenne pepper

Handful of chopped coriander (cilantro) and dill

Juice of ½ lemon

Sugar to taste (optional)

Toast the seeds lightly in a dry frying pan, grind to a powder using a pestle and mortar, and set aside. Slash the underside of the whole plums with a cross then put them in a large saucepan filled with boiling water and simmer over a medium heat until they start to break down slightly and are very soft (this entirely depends on the ripeness of your plums, slide in a knife to check). Remove, allow to cool, and take out the stones – don't bother removing the skins though – and purée in a blender. Add the ground spices, garlic, salt, cayenne pepper, fresh herbs and lemon juice, and pulse a few times to combine everything. Check the seasoning, if it is too sour, add a good pinch of sugar, and give it a thorough stir.

Once entirely cool, transfer to a sterilised jar, seal and refrigerate where it'll keep for a week.

# Coriander Soup for All Seasons

This soup is inspired by one served at the Vinotel in Tbilisi, where it is poured over a single piece of thin dark rye bread. I've eaten it in the winter indoors in the hotel's little sitting room filled with rugs and books, and outside in the garden on warmer days. Therefore, I am confident in suggesting it as a soup for all seasons, though obviously it is only good for lovers of coriander, that most divisive of herbs.

**SERVES 4**

2 tbsp olive oil

1 large onion, chopped

1 leek, chopped

2 large garlic cloves, chopped

½ tsp ground turmeric

½ tsp chilli powder

1 large potato, chopped

Sea salt and freshly ground black pepper

1 litre/4⅓ cups chicken stock

15g/½oz coriander (cilantro) leaves and stalks, roughly chopped

**TO SERVE**

4 thin slices of dark rye bread, toasted well

½ tsp red pepper flakes

Heat the oil in a large casserole over a medium heat and cook the onion and leek until soft and glossy, at least 15 minutes. Add the garlic and spices and stir for a minute or two. Tip in the potato and coat, stirring for 2 minutes, then season and add the stock and bring to the boil. Cook for 20 minutes, until the potato is soft. Add the coriander, cook for 5 minutes more, then, using a stick blender, blitz until smooth. When ready to serve, place a single piece of toasted rye bread in the base of each bowl, pour over the soup, then dust with red pepper flakes.

# Gozinaki and Cinnamon Ice Cream

The Cone Culture converted me, an ice-cream sceptic, into a fan. Their kiosk in central Tbilisi serves up brilliantly imaginative flavours and I have two firm favourites: firstly, mandarin and secondly, cinnamon and gozinaki (nut brittle).

For sure they don't make the latter like this recipe but this is a 'version of', and it does have the flavours and the wonderful nutty crunch of gozinaki. Best of all it doesn't require a machine. Before you're ready to scoop, let it soften a bit at room temperature.

**MAKES A 500ML/17FL OZ TUB**

80g/2¾oz Gozinaki (see recipe on page 139)

200g/7oz condensed milk

300ml/1¼ cups plus 1 tbsp double (heavy) cream

¼ tsp vanilla extract

½ tsp ground cinnamon, freshly ground if possible

Crumble the gozinaki, best you can as it is very sticky, into a bowl and set aside, reserving a little for later. Put the condensed milk, cream and vanilla into a large bowl and stir in the cinnamon. Using an electric hand mixer, move around the bowl slowly until it thickens; this will take up to a couple of minutes. Next, stir through the crumbled gozinaki, keeping a walnut-sized amount aside. Using a spatula, scrape into a freezer container, crumble the reserved gozinaki on the top (this looks nice; it is not an essential step), cover with a lid and freeze until firm, around 3–4 hours. Eat within a couple of weeks as homemade ice cream doesn't have the longevity of shop-bought stuff.

# MANDARINS IN THE SNOW

Every hike is a new beginning. A fresh shot at things. A crisp page. An opportunity to walk out, and into, the world, anew. But, I admit, sometimes it takes a degree of stubborn hope, and not least when it is snowing and –20°C. The nine-hour drive to Upper Svaneti in northwest Georgia had been interesting but thankfully not drama-filled. It was only once we were really climbing the heights when snow had turned the road to a pudding-like mix of melt and mud, that I found myself gripping the armrest a bit tighter as we skirted sheer drops.

Our journey, westwards towards the Black Sea and then northwards, had begun on David Agmashenebeli Avenue, where my friend Amelia introduced me to Dimitri Maisuradze, a semi-retired English-speaking engineer, and occasional chauffeur, who had worked in Svaneti. Instantly likeable, charming and calm, and a master of the Georgian shrug – even more pronounced than the Gallic version – Dimitri would stay with us for the duration, as guide and driver. We settled into his comfortable 4x4 Ford, alongside five litres of his family wine, colour of apple juice, which he'd decanted into a single large water bottle. Whatever the road had in store for us, we'd not go thirsty.

With so far to travel in one day, we all agreed not to stop often, but the village of Surami, 130 kilometres from Tbilisi, demanded a halt. It was the smell that enticed us. The main road was entirely dominated by bakeries all selling the same thing: nazuki, a flat chestnut-brown raisin bread the shape of a child's skateboard, which smelled tantalisingly of freshly baked hot cross buns. We paid for two and tore pieces off until, just forty minutes later, we reached the village of Ubisa with its monastic complex that Amelia, who'd been before, insisted I saw. A quick shrug from Dmitri that told us he was happy to stop for another cigarette break, and with that, we wandered in. The exterior, made from local stone, was Mediterranean-looking, and its four-storey tower dated back to the 12th century. Inside, we met the priest, another Dimitri, dressed in a pale blue and gold vestment who stood in front of frescoes which he told us had been wiped clean, below hip height, by goats that would wander in to lick the walls in search of salt (all God's creatures and all that). Higher up, 14th-century murals, unaffected by goats, were Byzantine in style, depicting Christ's crucifixion, Palm Sunday and the last supper. The air in the church was of unaired rugs and the incense of countless ages.

Once we were close to the Black Sea, where citrus grows freely, one more reason to stop presented itself: buckets of mandarins, sold right by the orchard where they grew. The seller was especially cheerful, insisting we see the trees up-close and meet his 'English spaniel'. I bought three kilos.

From there, we crept northwards towards the mountains. At one junction, a woman laden with containers of water jumped in for a lift. She explained that her pipes had failed since new ones were put in. Dimitri joked that it is when improvements are made, that things tend to go wrong. It was after we'd gone past the ginormous Enguri Dam that we entered Svaneti, and, in doing so, crossed a cultural and geographical gulf. Suddenly, everything was the colour of Christmas trees or else ice-cool blue. It turned bitterly cold. Waterfalls appeared as shattered blocks of metre-long silvery icicles, hanging like daggers. Massive vertiginous banks of pines and firs covered with hoarfrost met the hard jagged grey peaks of the Caucasus, all dusted with white veins of snow. Heavy clouds suggested more snow.

Finally, we drove into Mestia, the tourist hub of Upper Svaneti province, at dusk. The ancient stone watchtowers, the earliest dating back a thousand years, were visible in the gloom, formidable-looking.

For hundreds of years the Svan lived according to a medieval feudal system and unwritten law, including blood revenge whereby a serious insult would result in killing either the offender, or their male relative, which would then in turn be avenged by the murdered man's family creating a cycle of violence that could last generations. This ancient justice code existed up until the Soviet Union and there are more benign versions of it still today. The Soviet impact came relatively late to Svaneti due to resistance and the lack of roads. Before that era, there were only paths for riding or walking down and out of the valleys.

That night, by a log burner at the comfortable guesthouse, the three of us drank Dmitri's family wine. The huge plastic bottle had been wedged, immediately on arrival, into the kitchen refrigerator taking up half the space ('do you think they'll mind?' I asked Dmitri, to which I got a smile and a shrug in reply). We made plans for the next day. Unless a blizzard made it impossible, we'd take a cable car up the mountains for a short ridge walk. But all anticipation was tied up with Lamproba the following night, the tradition of lighting birch branches in the bitter darkness, remembering those departed, and pouring out the good drinks of Georgia, that is wine and chacha, onto snowy graves.

## A WALK ON THE ZURULDI RIDGE

The following morning, from Mestia we headed upwards aboard the Hatsvali cable car, past skiers, mainly young Georgians and Russians dressed in vintage ski wear, agreeing that our shared ambition was simple: prime views of the queen of the Caucasus, Mount Ushba.

Located in the southern spur of the Caucasus mountain range it borders both Russia and Georgia and has long captivated the best alpinists. Dates around a full moon are said to provide better climbing days but because Ushba is part of a massif that is one of the highest and most glaciated parts of the Caucasus the weather is infamously bad and changeable, so much so that some climbers call it the 'Rotten Corner' because of its unpredictability. Captivating and bleak, feared and admired, Mount Ushba has taken the lives of many excellent mountaineers.

At the top of the Zuruldi ridge we began to head east, walking at about 2,400 metres. There were signposts for fair weather hikes and a map pinned to a board, but, given the intense winter weather and knee-deep snow, we decided to just set out in the direction of an old transmitter used as a marker, to see how far as we could go. Walking was hard on the legs, but with gaiters on, it was possible.

Hunchbacked by my rucksack we went on, looking for the best view of Mount Ushba whenever breaks in the treeline came. Its distinctive pair of peaks are the reason why to the Svan people Ushba is 'the undividable'. The sight of it, with thin clouds drifting across it like a scarf, directly opposite from the valley far below, was so unutterably beautiful that my eyes almost refused it. Snowbound Ushba is truly heartstopping. Cold as it was, tiring as it was to walk through such deep virgin snow, it was impossible, with such a view, to wish instead for gentle summertime with its easier walking, flowers, green alpine slopes and cattle on hillsides.

At one particularly advantageous point, we stopped and I handed around some mandarins. Taking our padded gloves off, we ate at least three each. What bliss it was to taste them with Ushba as company.

## 'THE SPIRIT OF THE HILL IS NOT OF THIS WORLD'

English travellers, mainly male and Eton-educated, became interested in the Caucasus during the second half of the 19th century, the 'silver age of alpinism' a term given to the era in mountaineering that began with Edward Whymper's ascent of the Matterhorn in the Alps in 1865. This was when climbers such as Douglas Freshfield scaled Elbrus (5,642 metres) in the western part of the Caucasus. The celebrated surgeon and mountaineer Clinton Thomas Dent went, and returned with glowing reviews of climbing in the Caucasus to share with the Alpine Club.

Freshfield, in his travel account, wrote of how Svaneti was an unknown playground for mountaineers, but how by 1920 he expected 'Svanetians will have begun to collect crystals and to make bouquets of yellow lilies… and the village headsman will have a roll of porters and a tariff for the Tuiber and Zanner Passes'. He needn't have feared: revolutions and Communism sealed off the region for decades to outsiders. His belief was that we ought to count the world's great mountains 'among the glories of the world' and that isn't hard to agree with but there was a distinct arrogance to the climbing men of that era. Nonetheless, Freshfield's two-volume book, *The Exploration of the Caucasus*, is notable not just as a historic document, and because it triggered huge interest in the Caucasus among European climbers, but because it contains images by the Italian photographer and legendary alpinist Vittorio Sella. He arranged expeditions to the Caucasus in the late 19th century for which he was awarded prizes by Tsar Nicholas II and London's Royal Geographical Society. Sella's black and white images can be seen at Mestia's Museum of History and Ethnography, one of the largest treasuries of Georgian history and an outstanding small museum that has received accolades worldwide.

A lot has been written of these mountain men but less so about Joyce Dunsheath. Born in Norwich, England, in 1902, Dunsheath gained a rare and hard-to-get permit to visit the Caucasus in 1957 as her husband, Percy, was invited to an international electro-technical conference in Russia. She wrote of her adventures in *Guest of the Soviets* (1959) and in the *Ladies' Alpine Club Journal*.

Dunsheath was a purist. Mountaineering was an activity that ought to be free from competition, 'a sport to be enjoyed… to harden the body and learn the skills which will make for success… each one matching her own strength against the strength of the mountain… those gaining the summit know that the spirit of the hill is not of this world,' as she eloquently wrote.

By October 1957 she'd made a bid for Mount Elbrus, the highest of the Caucasus range, and generally accepted to also be Europe's tallest but that depends on where the frontiers are drawn. She was the only woman with a team of Russian climbers and interpreters and a meteorologist who'd been stationed on Elbrus during the war. They made it to the top, clad in masks to save their faces from frostbite.

'Linking arms, we passed the summit cairn without stopping and did not pause till we were within the shelter of rocks well below the top. Darkness fell before we reached the refuge at the end of a fourteen-hour day of non-stop struggle with the elements. We had won, and I was satisfied …'

From there, Dunsheath's group crossed into Georgia via the Becho Pass and into Upper Svaneti. 'The next day we reached Mestia (Seti), capital of Svanetia: "Free Svanetia" it is rightly called – in spite of all attempts to subdue it by Romans, Persians, Turks, Georgians and Russians, it maintained its independence right up to 1875. Shut in between towering mountain walls, Svanetia still feels little of the impact of civilisation and cares nothing for the politics of Moscow.'

Throughout history Svan people haven't cared much for outside rulers generally and it worked both ways. The Soviets saw mountainous regions as places of backwardness adverse to the project of socialist advancement. This was illustrated by the 55-minute silent movie *Salt for Svanetia*, first shown in 1931, which depicted Svans as superstitious and primitive, and lacking in even the most basic essentials, namely salt. The film opens by quoting Lenin: 'Even now there are far reaches of the Soviet Union where the patriarchal way of life persists along with remnants of the clan system.' Three years after the film premiered, a road was built connecting Svaneti to the rest of the world.

Dunsheath recounted a memorable family meal in Mestia: 'We had a feast of cold chicken which was divided into the requisite number of portions and eaten with the fingers, sour milk in a central bowl into which each dipped his spoon, and potatoes steamed in their jackets. Many were the toasts proposed and drunk in the home-brewed vodka …' Later, she mentions, with well-meaning transliteration, being 'invited to share the family supper of "hatchipoury"' (Georgia's famous cheese-filled breads).

Her obituary in *The Alpine Journal* detailed her later in life accomplishments – in her sixties she gained an A level in Russian, along with her other activities namely 'the bassoon and the flute with the local orchestra. She was a generous and kindly person, always willing to help when help was needed, and an enthusiastic gardener.' Today, Joyce Dunsheath's photographic portrait is held in London's National Portrait Gallery, taken the year before she travelled to the Caucasus. From what I've read, I imagine I would have liked her.

Thinking about these climbers, and breathing in the divine freshness of the snowy ridge, I beetled along on our own comparatively modest stroll, each one of us walking in a line and staring out across the valley towards

Ushba with its magnificent wolf-ear peaks. We were solar-powered simply by the sight of the great mountain but given the depth of the snow, managed to cover only five kilometres or so there and back.

## RICH FATS, BEER AND WINE

Walking is itself a form of enquiry, highlighting our interdependence both on one another and our environment. But mountains and the countryside, often viewed as natural, simple and unchanging are none of these things in reality. While the beauty of such nature cannot be denied, it is important not to romanticise, or fictionalise, peaks and valleys. They are managed and settled. Helicopters, and drones, can reach the remotest parts, so can mountaineers. On the ridge, we saw rotating blades high above us carrying risk-taking heli-skiers. Mountains are not simply 'scenery' they are intrinsic, essential, elemental. By indulging such notions, which are extremely easy to fall into when met with such vistas, we risk othering the inhabitants of remote places as well. This can be seen not only historically in the diaries and books of English mountaineers and Russian writers, such as Lermontov and Tolstoy, but in the attitude of city dwellers with greater political powers today.

That evening, in a warm and cosy tavern that smelled of deliciously fatty meats, beer and wine, I wondered what to eat. The Svan menu is slightly different from elsewhere in Georgia. Soup featured, obviously, but there was also pan-fried chvishtari, small flatbreads made with local green millet and cheese, shaped in an oval about the size of a saucer. Greasy and crispy on the outside, with a slightly vinegary or fermented scent, chvishtari is exactly what you need with a high mountain snowstorm whirling just beyond the door.

I slept well that night, thinking of how fortunate we were to have warm beds in such weather. And as I drifted off I remembered what Tamara, the charming Svan lady who ran the guesthouse we slept in, had told me: that once the Svan would rely on huge bundles of cannabis to keep warm – they'd burn it in fires in their homes for the purpose of aiding sleep in the bitter cold.

# Chvishtari – Small Mountain Cheese Breads

Chvishtari was the first thing I ate in Mestia, Svaneti, during the deep bitter winter. Made with a rare local green millet, it arrived at the table sizzlingly hot and about the size of my hand. It was cheesy, a little greasy and deliciously moreish. This interpretation, made with maize meal – which is found in health food shops or larger supermarkets – is an ideal accompaniment for any sort of soup.

**MAKES 4**

50ml/3 tbsp whole milk

1 egg, beaten

¼ tsp white wine vinegar

160g/about 1 cup maize meal (cornmeal)

70g/½ cup self-raising flour

½ tsp salt

80g/2¾oz feta, crumbled

80g/2¾oz mozzarella, thinly sliced

2 tbsp vegetable oil

In a large mixing bowl combine the milk with the beaten egg and vinegar, then slowly tip in the flours and salt, stirring as you go. Incorporate the cheeses into the mix. The dough mixture will be wet and like very thick pancake batter.

Divide the dough into four pieces and, on a lightly floured surface, shape them into ovals about 1cm/½in thick. You may need to cook in batches, depending on the size of the pan. Heat 2 tablespoons of oil in a large frying pan and, when very hot, let them cook over a medium heat for 5 minutes or so, then turn over and cook for another 5. You want them golden. Repeat until all four are cooked. Ideally serve warm – though they reheat well, fried in a pan again.

# WANDERING AMONG THE DEAD: MEAT PIES AND BURNING BIRCH

The next morning, at dawn on Valentine's Day, the moon was a perfect half in the sky. Feeling truly in the mountains again, I sat bundled in a blanket on the wooden balcony watching as snow billowed off the hilltops merging with clouds. Tonight would be Lamproba.

A power cut had wiped out the electricity all night which didn't bother me as when moving closer to nature you have to re-accustom yourself to the unexpected. Mainly I felt relief, imagining how, high above Mestia, up in the remotest hills, it would be utterly silent, the only noise occasionally coming from avalanches, animals and birds. Shut off from the rest of the world by the mountains' immense stature, you can feel them begin to silently possess you. It is not an unpleasant sensation.

All around stood the old Svan defence towers, stretching skywards, and in the tiny lanes mountain dogs had left behind their lion-sized pawprints in the snow. The towers, usually with three to five floors, are as tall as 25 metres, with an entrance above ground accessed by a ladder that could be pulled up during an attack. These mini-fortresses, where in times of threat whole families would retreat with their holy icons, are to do with both warring clans and outsiders. Joyce Dunsheath knew this when she wrote, 'These usually were not the enemy from a foreign land but the next-door neighbour out to avenge insult by murder.' A striking black and white photograph, taken by Vittorio Sella, in Mestia's excellent museum, shows an old Svan house with bear paws hanging ominously on its facade, a sign of hunting and a warning. Skinned, they look just like human hands.

Not so long ago, it was considered dangerous to come to Svaneti so lawless was it, and the chances of robbery were high. Mestia nowadays, popular with skiers in winter and hikers in summer, has different issues. Most obviously the strains that come with tourism but also criminality around cryptocurrency mining which causes the power cuts. Since a government-led programme of subsidised electricity to mountain regions was introduced, with the aim of keeping remote communities alive, some have been using the discounted power to create virtual money which means hotels, cafés and restaurants, all the things that prop up Svaneti's much-needed tourism, suffer from frequent outages.

Quietly walking downstairs in the gloom, I could see that despite a lack of electricity somehow Tamara had laid out a generous buffet of bread, jam, boiled eggs, Georgian kiwis and fresh coffee, too. A group of photographers from Florence came downstairs to eat, chattering about how they hadn't felt safe on the roads coming up, which made me grateful again for Dimitri's solid car and careful driving. I baulked when they told me they hoped to fly a drone over tonight's mournful Lamproba gathering. It was that uncomfortable seesaw again: the jarring impact of tourism and the mix of guilt, naivety and manipulation it creates.

After breakfast, a walk through the backstreets led me past huge wooden doors, carved with local scenery of medieval towers and mountains, and shops offering Svan salt (a punchy flavoured salt combining spices such as blue fenugreek and marigold) and horses to rent. Quite a different place to the one Dunsheath visited in the 1950s when she noted: 'Mestia is proud of being up to date and, although it has no sanitation, boasts a post office from which telegrams can be sent in the Russian and Georgian languages and a primitive hotel for the convenience of the occasional traveller.'

Snow fell silently, the only noise came from a drove of hairy-backed pigs and their litter of piglets, busily snouting about. At the foot of the town, the river ran like liquid silver. All we had to do now was wait for evening to come. At the churches, the wood had already been chopped and the birch bundles were piled next to the tombs.

**A BATTLE OF ICE AND HEAT**

That night, Amelia, Dimitri and I arrived at the small village of Lenjeri, close to Mestia, where we were staying, but also a world away. In the graveyard, men went past us speaking Svan. Kevin Tuite, the Caucasian linguistics professor, noted that the Svan language 'is no closer to Georgian than Icelandic is to Modern English'. It is said there are fewer than 15,000 Svan speakers left, therefore hearing it felt like an honour. Through powdery snow they marched with bundles of wood flung over shoulders, the thin birch branches a metre long, flames billowing like auburn hair behind them.

It was 8p.m. and Lamproba would continue late into the night. After a day where the temperature had dropped again to −20°C, we stood quietly as it grew even colder and I quickly lost the feeling in my fingers despite thick gloves. Snow came halfway up our legs. Some of the older village men wore traditional grey Svan felt hats, round and with black seams on their top forming a cross (a symbol that says 'may the cross protect you').

One gravestone next to me, etched with a portrait of a man wearing a black wool chokha, a warrior coat with elongated cartridge holders or kilas on the chest, looked frighteningly combustible lined as it was with plastic bottles filled with chacha and candles. At another graveside, a young woman poured red wine onto the surrounding snow, then set down a tray containing a fruit platter of kiwis and mandarins, several boiled eggs and three flat kubdari, Svan meat pies, the size and shape of dinner plates.

Soon enough, we were joined by Vakhtang Pilpani, who introduced himself, in English, as a villager of Lenjeri and the leader of an ensemble of polyphonic singers called Riho ('early morning'). This legendary group, of several dozen men, is well-known and the village contains many Pilpani family members. Their job, he told us, is to keep the tradition of ancient Svan songs alive, some of which are believed to date back several hundred years. They are not so much members of a choir, he continued, they are 'simply Svan'.

'Here, please take this domestic wine,' he smiled, handing me a cup. With his dog, a golden ball of hip-height fluff, at his side, he smiled generously and set about schooling us.

'How does Lamproba work? Well, there is one fire from one family for somebody who has died,' he began. 'Usually it will be for someone who was lost recently, or too young. We are Orthodox Christian but this tradition predates Christianity. There are many connections to fire in this valley. Once the armies of Tamerlane came to Svaneti, nobody was coming here then, there were no roads, and so we were mainly left alone and didn't have enemies. Our people came to the border to meet this army and everyone took not one but two fires each. Therefore, while it was a thousand people, it looked like two thousand. They retreated. Two weeks ago we marked this event, we sang and danced around the church, celebrating with fire.'

Strabo, the ancient geographer born in Amasya (ancient Amaseia, now in the Black Sea region of Turkey) in 64 BCE, wrote in his *Geography* about the Svan, known in classical sources as Soanes. As the museum in Mestia explained: 'Soanes are superior perhaps to all the tribes in strength and courage. They are masters of the country around them, and occupy the heights of the Caucasus ... all their people are fighting men ...'

We asked Pilpani if there is a chance of the tradition of Lamproba dying out.

'No. People like to remember and young people will continue it as they also miss those who died. We have funeral days, we sing our songs, and that lives on in every village.' Dogs barked into the night as more fires lit up around the black valley, highlighting where villagers, not forgotten, lay buried. I later read that up until the 1950s there were 160 feast days in Upper Svaneti.

Pilpani went on to tell us about life in the valley. How each hamlet was built around nine kilometres apart from another to ensure that there was enough land to graze and grow for everyone.

'Our people have always led a strong, very active physical life in fresh air. No sugar, and every day fresh milk. No Coca-Cola, no crisps. That is why we live a long time. My grandmother was 102, my great-great-grandfather, 106.'

I wanted to know if the secret to long life, quite common throughout the Caucasus, was kefir as some claim.

'They didn't drink kefir, they drank chacha and they ate bread. Maybe a little vodka. By the way, we have always been happy when people from another place come to see us, it was like news, like BBC. In Georgia hospitality is our big tradition, and this continues. Here, please take some kubdari or khachapuri. You must try.'

The cold did not seem to faze any of the villagers, filled with wine and chacha, though my toes ached with it. Even children, round as bowling balls in puffa jackets, seemed unaware. I was transfixed by the village dogs that weaved through the graves somehow knowing to stay away from the graveside foods and the plastic cups of wine wedged into the snow. Towers glowed from the fires lit beneath them, all around the valley. I lost count of how many.

We thanked the villagers and moved out, passing more ornamental gravestones, crafted to appear like mini defensive towers complete with door, windows and portraits, to another graveyard along the valley, which locals called Raana.

From the road, the cemetery was lit by dozens of fires throwing sparks up into the sky, flashes of hand torches and embers flaring in hollows like small volcanoes. A battle of ice and heat. Power had returned, a church glowed a sickly yellow in the distance, but it was nevertheless incredibly hard to walk on such deep snow in the dark. In the graveyard, mandarins, chocolates, roast meats, khachapuri, kubdari, bottles and bottles of chacha were being pulled out of shopping bags for graveside picnics in the snow, by the birch bonfires.

At the perimeter, beside a dry-stone wall, a large group of men had gathered around the tomb of one man who'd died young in a car crash. That was in 1988,

Dimitri said. But here they were, still coming every year. Sat in a circle, they were talking, sharing food and laughing, as if in a pub. It was moving to witness, and I thought to myself: what could be a nicer way to be remembered? That your friends gather beside you, to include you once again, long after you'd gone. 'It's like they've come to tell him their news. They're talking to him,' Dimitri said. 'Death is not only a bad thing, he has gone to God.'

We stopped by one artistically set tray of grapes, apples and kubdari, a thin church candle set in the middle like a birthday cake, a small glass of amber wine put in the snow next to it. The flicking fires, in pits shovelled free of snow, reflected in the polished black granite headstones, many engraved with portraits and the Georgian flag, giving the appearance of movement in life and death.

## WINE FOR LONELY GRAVES

To the sound of clinking glasses we walked on, meeting faces lit in fiery hues of bronze and orange and going past some tombs that were tended only by a single person, often old, often praying, while at others as many as a dozen people gathered. Some shared plates of chocolate wafers and sweets, others chicken drumsticks, perhaps favourite foods of the departed, perhaps what happened to have been cooked at home that day. A meal to share with friends, and the dead, either way. As we walked, losing our footing in the dark and the snow, it was hard to know where some of the graves were and I suffered an acute nervousness of where to stand. As I'd seen others do, I poured a little wine on some of the lonelier graves.

Back in Mestia, at the church of St George, a woman dressed in a beautiful black fur coat and beret and with immaculate make-up, pushed a huge slice of chocolate cake into my hand. 'Chocolate torte. Delicious!' She said, with a smile, in Russian. 'Very! Very!' How could I refuse? She was in her sixties, she explained, and was at the grave of her parents, her mother had passed away aged 90 the previous year. She told us her surname was Khergiani, a name belonging to a family of climbers, the most celebrated being Mikhail Khergiani. An unexpected but neat link to the following day's adventure.

# Svan Bloody Mary

In Tbilisi, at a bar named Politika (currently closed), it used to be possible to order an ingenious twist on the classic Bloody Mary whereby the glass would be rimmed with deeply savoury Svan salt. Bear in mind this is punchy stuff with garlic and blue fenugreek so a light touch is best here. It is ideal as a brunch cocktail.

**MAKES 1 COCKTAIL**

Svan salt (see page 248)

Ice cubes

200ml/scant 1 cup tomato juice

40ml/2½ tbsp vodka

A few shakes of Tabasco, to taste

Squeeze of lemon juice

Sparingly, rim a large glass with Svan salt (one way to do this is to lightly wet the rim of the glass with water then upend it on a saucerful of salt). Add the ice. Pour over the tomato juice, vodka, then season to taste with Tabasco and lemon juice, and stir or muddle well.

# Kubdari – Meaty Flatbreads from Svaneti

Kubdari is essentially a large and hearty flatbread with a thinnish filling of well-spiced meat. Here I've used beef but you could also use pork. These are a little smaller than is traditional but they are still large enough to make for a decent lunch, or else can be wrapped and put into a rucksack.

A note on the spices used here. If you have Svan salt (see page 248) – which typically combines salt, coriander, blue fenugreek, dried marigold petals, garlic, red pepper and caraway seeds – then use 1–1½ tablespoons of that (the salt mixes vary, and some are very pungent, so you will need to judge this a little) instead of the individual spices, but do add a little extra red pepper and paprika.

These are best served warm straight from the oven, brushed with some butter, but are absolutely fine at room temperature too. They might be, as my friend and recipe tester Giverny pointed out, great for a picnic, too.

**MAKES 4**

**FOR THE DOUGH**

275g/2 cups plain (all-purpose) flour, plus extra for dusting

7g/¼oz fast-action dried yeast

1 tsp fine sea salt

1 tsp caster (superfine) sugar

125g/generous ½ cup natural yogurt

1 egg, beaten

Butter, to serve

**FOR THE FILLING**

2 tbsp vegetable oil

1 small onion, diced

1 large garlic clove, crushed

1 tbsp ground coriander

1 tsp blue fenugreek

2 tsp sweet paprika

1 tsp red pepper flakes

1 tsp dill seeds (optional)

1 tbsp tomato purée (paste)

350g/12oz minced (ground) beef

Sea salt and freshly ground pepper

Put the flour into a large bowl, adding the yeast to one side and the salt and sugar on the other. Stir through the yogurt and add 6 tablespoons of lukewarm water. Mix until you have a shaggy dough, then tip it out onto a lightly floured surface and knead until soft and silky, about 10 minutes. Form it into a ball, place in a lightly oiled mixing bowl and cover with a damp tea towel. Leave to rise in a warm place for about 1–1½ hours.

When the dough has almost doubled in size, prepare the filling. Warm
1 tablespoon of the oil in a frying pan over a medium heat and stir-fry the
onion until soft and starting to colour, then add the garlic, all the spices,
then the remaining tablespoon of oil, the tomato purée and finally, the beef,
seasoning with ½ tsp of salt. Continue to stir-fry until cooked through,
8–10 minutes. Remove from the heat and allow to cool.

Once the mince is cool, preheat the oven to 200°C/400°F/gas mark 6 and line
2 baking trays. Divide the dough into four pieces and shape into balls, keeping
those you aren't working with under a damp tea towel to avoid drying out. Lightly
dust your surface with flour, and roll out one ball of dough into a 20cm/8in
round. Place a quarter of the filling in the middle of the round then stretch and
fold in the dough towards the centre, shaping like a money bag, then flip it over,
seam side down. Pat it gently, shaping with your hands, or very lightly using
a rolling pin until you have a round, flat filled bread, about 14cm/5½in. Repeat
the process with the remaining balls. When they are all rolled out, brush each
one with beaten egg and sprinkle over a few sea salt flakes and a couple of
grinds of fresh black pepper.

Bake for 25–30 minutes until the top is golden all over (if you're baking on
2 racks in the oven, switch halfway through so all four bake equally). When ready,
brush with a little butter and serve warm (best), or at room temperature (fine).

# MOUNTAIN TIGERS
# AND DAZZLING ALPINISTS

A silent, cow-filled lane led me from Mestia to its outskirts where a foreboding 10th-century stone house stood alone wrapped in a vapour of heavy snow. I slouched towards the wooden door, past a solemn bust atop a plinth in the courtyard confirming that I was at the right address, and knocked. No answer. I called the telephone number, as listed online, and to my surprise a man picked up. He was the nephew of the legendary climber, Mikhail Khergiani, confusingly with exactly the same first and last name. Kindly, he offered to come and unlock the home of his forebears, now a museum, right away.

As I'd guessed from meeting other Khergianis at the Lamproba gatherings the previous night, the name was not uncommon locally. Two of the most notable, Beknu and Gabriel Khergiani, were part of the team that removed the Nazi flag from the peak of Elbrus in 1943 after it had been placed there by German troops. As for Mikhail Khergiani, the alpinist born in this house in 1932, and buried in Mestia, he was one of the greatest Soviet climbers of any decade – the 'tiger of the cliffs' as he became known – his ascents and bravery, legendary.

Mikhail arrived quickly as promised, bundled up in a hat and jangling a huge set of old keys, leading the way out of the snow and into a large rustic room on the ground floor of the old machubi (traditional Svan house). This was, he explained, where twenty or so people would sleep in winter. The extended family would bundle together onto a large shelf above a series of wooden arched nooks, each one built to house an individual cow, to keep warm. Above this clever arrangement a giant flat stone panel hung from the roof which the fire below would warm, thus heating the room more. An early form of radiator.

Opposite, on the stone wall, family portraits were displayed by a wooden Svanetian throne, placed before the hearth, used by the head of the family. Typically Svan, the room not only mirrored agricultural life but also its traditional honour codes. In some machubi homes, Mikhail said, there would be a dungeon for keeping prisoners.

The galleries of Mestia's excellent museum are filled with displays of magical things: 'sheepbird' pendants (ram's head, a bird's body) dating back to 2500 BCE, and 'stones of sin' that were hung around the neck of wrongdoers. Also, a gigantic ancient ritual cauldron, specially made for cooking sacrificed animals, crafted by a coppersmith who'd welded together 52 sheets of copper precisely to be fastened with rivets. It was, visitors are told, kept in the village square and was very costly to rent, the equivalent of a whole day's wage. Perhaps the most moving artefact in the museum was the Svanetian shimekvshe ('broken arm') musical instrument, similar to a harp and linked to a tragic legend: a father who'd lost his only son in war, had made the instrument from his son's arm, attaching his golden hair as strings. And with this, he played mournful melodies day and night.

Of Svanetian crafts, and writing, it is said that 'the hands of workers decay but their work remains as treasure', a truism which can also be applied to the valley's alpinists.

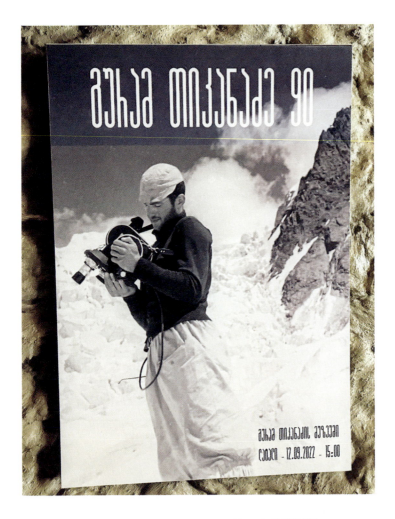

At Khergiani's house, we slowly moved through the rooms displaying everything to do with the great climber, his ropes, his stoves, notebooks, badges and trophies. Portraits of him covered almost every inch of the walls, many showing him in a CCCP (Union of Soviet Socialist Republics) branded tracksuit with his Svan family in traditional clothes. As a climber, Khergiani was not just representing Svaneti or Georgia, but the entire Soviet Union, often travelling abroad for international competitions and taking part in exchanges with other foreign alpinists. The world of Soviet climbing was one that endorsed high risk, and Upper Svaneti, where people are born in the mountains and know well life at high altitude, predictably produced many outstanding alpinists.

'I was fascinated by the successes of my uncle and father – they climbed Ushba. I made my decision as a child – only alpinism, nothing more,' reads one quote hanging above a rucksack and a primitive camping stove. His father, Vissarion, who also summited Ushba, was head of the Mountain Rescue Service of Mestia and made more than a hundred ascents of mountains in the Caucasus.

Standing in Khergiani's bedroom, complete with single bed and a smiling portrait where a pillow would be, it was impossible to think of these men and not to also consider what they attempted, and accomplished, without the aid of modern weather forecasting or the sort of technical crampons, helmets and axes used by today's climbers. The old-style equipment often failed them. Ropes tore (nylon ropes for climbers came about only in the 1950s) and wooden handles of ice axes broke. Traditionally, Svan climbers would insulate their shoes with a local grass named tserkwa.

In one room, filled with trophies, hangs the red rope that Khergiani was attached to when he fell to his death, aged just 37. In 1969, at the peak of his career, he travelled to the Italian Dolomites as part of an official Soviet expedition and exchange. Climbing a challenging wall on the infamous Su-Alto peak, he'd cleared the hardest stretch but then came rock fall, not only hitting him but severing his climbing ropes. He fell to his death. The tragedy was felt by climbing communities worldwide and was marked by the Soviet superstar singer-songwriter Vladimir Vysotsky, with his song 'To the Top', while the poet Yevgeny Yevtushenko wrote 'The Rope of Khergiani'.

His death left behind his widow Kato 'but no children', Mikhail said with sadness before adding that while he'd never met his uncle – he had died a year before he was born – he had been named after him in his memory.

The museum to this great climber warrants the long drive to Mestia alone, so atmospheric and well looked after is it. But while a simple phone call had opened the door to Khergiani's museum, it would be a little harder to gain access to another, far less known, museum dedicated to another of Georgia's great climbers, the alpinist Guram Tikanadze. A contemporary of Khergiani, I had heard that a memorial museum had also been dedicated to him in the village of Latali, not far from Mestia. Dimitri agreed to help, it was too far to walk in the deep snow, and we set off.

## ESCAPING THE SOVIET PRISON BOX

Again and again Dimitri stopped villagers to ask for directions to the museum of Guram Tikanadze but we were met only with puzzlement. Then just as we were about to give up, one man said he did know and pointed down a track towards a stone house with thick snow up the windows. The top floor of the Guram Tikanadze Sports Centre and Museum, where the displays were, was locked. Dimitri set off to investigate and I waited in a hall, well below freezing, where a hardy group of children were practising judo. There was no electricity again and a single stove did what it could in the corner. After half an hour or so, Dimitri returned with a man who would unlock the museum and we made our way upstairs, breath billowing.

Tikanadze, not born in Svaneti but at lower elevations, in a village in Guria by the Black Sea, was an excellent and celebrated climber as well as an acclaimed photojournalist providing images to Czech and Polish publications. Best remembered locally as 'the first Georgian photographer known to the world across the Iron Curtain', photography was his trade, mountaineering more of a hobby. But that is to downplay it. As a talented alpinist, he made forty ascents of perilous mountains and won silver medals for his climbing.

The museum, which is entered via a stunning carved Svan door, is being carefully looked after by the Parjiani family in the village. It is small but artfully put together with stone walls, a wooden ceiling and a glass armoire holding books and portraits. Tikanadze's strikingly good black and white photographs lined the walls, including one of a climb up Tetnuldi (4,858 metres) and the last picture he ever took of a Svan boy in the village of Ushguli. Also on show during my visit were a few colour photographs, likely from Uzbekistan or Tajikistan, of turbaned men with melons, and others drinking tea at a shaded outdoors chaikhana. In August 1963, Tikanadze died descending Shkhara (5,193 metres) on the Russia–Georgia border, east of Mestia. I do think Tikanadze, and this atmospheric small museum built in his name, deserves to be better known outside of the Caucasus. The first step could be a simple sign on the side of the road to help others find it and I hope before long one is put up.

As Mikhail, the nephew, had said at Khergiani's museum, climbing was a way to maintain some form of independence, to escape the 'prison box' of the Soviet Union. The magnetic pull of the mountains is strong enough today, but when crushed by the limitations of Soviet rule, with its rampant mistrust and absurd repressions, the appeal for those who were able to climb must have been immense.

As we left the museum, I considered my own humble walking plans. Svaneti in deep winter, when the going is not easy for those who live in the valleys with the challenges of frozen pipes and electricity blackouts, had made such an impression that I wanted to return in summer. Having seen the views, it was impossible not to.

# A Soup to Showcase Georgian Spices

As every cook knows, just one herb or spice can make all the difference to a dish, and in Georgia it is the ingenious use of spices, often creating a truly unusual flavour, that makes me really sit up. If you visit, you are almost certainly going to travel home with some spice packets in your luggage, maybe containing Svan salt, or the classic khmeli suneli mix (coriander seed, dried marigold petals, chilli pepper, blue fenugreek) or perhaps just some dried marigold flowers ('the herb of the sun'). And so, when armed with such delicacies, it is helpful to have a simple recipe that will happily take them on board, like this one.

**SERVES 4**

1 red onion, cut into wedges

1 red bell pepper, chopped

200g/7oz carrot, chopped

200g/7oz parsnip, chopped

200g/7oz peeled butternut squash, chopped

1 potato, chopped

2 garlic cloves, crushed

1½ tbsp olive oil

2 tsp khmeli suneli or 1 tsp Svan salt (see page 248)

Sea salt and freshly ground black pepper

1 litre/4⅓ cups chicken stock

Preheat the oven to 200°C/400°F/gas mark 6. Line a roasting tin with foil and add all of the vegetables and the garlic, drizzle over the oil, add the khmeli suneli or Svan salt, season well with salt (unless you are using Svan salt) and pepper, and mix. Roast for 35 minutes, giving the vegetables a stir halfway through. Once roasted, tip the lot into a large saucepan, pour in the hot stock, and simmer for about 5 minutes. Use a stick blender to purée the soup and check the seasoning. Serve with bread.

# STROLLING SUMMERTIME SVANETI: OLD GOLD AND ALPINE FLOWERS

'The earth laughs in flowers' wrote Ralph Waldo Emerson and, reawakened after such a long hard winter in Svaneti, it certainly does.

As planned, I returned in summer, with James this time, to walk and admire Mount Ushba again. We drove up from Tbilisi, the journey a cinch compared with deep winter. Lozenges of snow clung to hollows in the valleys but lower elevations were sheer green, as green as an English cricket pitch. Up high, the passes would still be bitter and icy as it was only the beginning of June, the very start of the season, but even so it was already busy with visitors, a sharp contrast to February. I'd just about managed to get us into the Grand Hotel Ushba, run partly by the remarkable Richard Baerug, a Norwegian writer and speaker of the Svan language who has lived in Svaneti for more than a decade and who has detailed, in books, dozens of trails he has skied and walked. We had just three nights and only because there had been a cancellation. The hotel, a comfortable, wooden chalet-style inn with the best view of Mount Ushba imaginable, is a well-known bridgehead for adventuring and is extremely popular with hikers.

When we stepped out of the car, under a Svan flag flapping on a pole, a cross on a yellow background, suddenly the smell of honeysuckle azaleas was everywhere. All around, the colours of summer glowed in the fresh mountain air. Red flowering sheep sorrel was so abundant that there were whole carpets of it while at the roadside, grape hyacinth and large daisies sprouted sunwards. After the long drive I sucked in lungfuls of air so clean that you don't just breathe it, you feel it and feel it to the point of being cleansed. As a couple of shaggy hip-height Svanetian dogs came to greet us, a herd of chestnut and white horses, followed by their foals, came down the valley, too, filling the path. What you choose to gaze upon – animals, rivers, mountains, valleys, fields of forget-me-nots – depends on who you are, and whether it is walking, fishing, botany or scaling peaks that enthrals. With the advent of warmer weather, all of these ways are open-ended again. Summer as promise, and possibility.

Sitting on the balcony, reviving ourselves with coffee and wine after the long drive, while enjoying the gentle clamour of nature all around, we made plans with Richard's book. One section discussed the ethics and claims around peak bagging and the conquering of mountains by foreign teams. While a Swiss-German-Austrian climbing party declared they'd made the first ascent of the southern summit of Ushba in 1903, as Richard points out, 'it is not impossible that Svan hunters or mountaineers went to the top in the 1800s or earlier'.

The next day, with one of Richard's guides, Beka Arghwlian from the nearby village of Twebish, we set out. A short drive up a steep winding road took us to a parking spot, by the Ughviri Pass which would have been all but impossible to reach in winter, and from there we walked a few kilometres to the village of Tsvirmi. The views opened up. Green valleys folding in on one another and behind them, taller white-capped mountains. Settled in between, scattered villages, with their distinctive defence towers.

Buttercups led the way to Tsvirmi's Church of the Saviour where Beka rang a villager who came with a key to unlock it. While it seemed unlikely anyone would dare plunder a holy place in Svaneti, it immediately became clear why, unlike many churches, it was securely locked.

We stepped into the cool silence of the church and once inside, all eyes were immediately drawn to a stack of gold- and silver-plated wooden crosses, leaning against one another by a blackened wall. Glowing reverently in the gloom, coloured by age and candle smoke, they had been engraved with friezes of saints on horseback. Each one, completely priceless, left alone in this secluded valley, safely locked away. Beka explained that they are likely not Svan but were probably brought up from lower Georgia for safekeeping during difficult periods of invasion.

'Svaneti was the last frontier, so it was considered safe,' he said. It made sense that with such valuable and precious contents, there was a Svan defence tower rising above the church.

The historian Christoph Baumer discusses gold in his book on the Caucasus stating that Svaneti was the northeastern hinterland of Colchis (a district of Asia Minor at the eastern extremity of the Black Sea and celebrated in Greek mythology as home of Medea and the destination of the Argonauts), before adding that even in prehistoric times, the Svan used sheepskins to wash gold dust from their rivers.

Some believe that Svaneti could be the biblical Eden and this is partly due to the abundance of gold deposits. The wealth of the Colchians, though, was mainly from fishing and agriculture, as well as metalwork.

Admiring the crosses, I thought back to the museum in Mestia, where a sign explained how Svaneti coins, considered treasures, were kept in churches, and how since ancient times there was a donation of coins to churches as a pledge of fortune, abundance and health.

'During the Soviet Union our churches were left alone but elsewhere in Georgia many were destroyed,' said the key holder, ushering a dog out who had followed us in. Back outside, Beka pointed to a nearby river and said that there is still much gold panning today.

**SVAN SALT WITH EVERYTHING**

As we walked through the village, Beka, a keen mountaineer himself, spoke about Svan culture. 'You know our old flag was not flat but shaped like a lion or a wolf, with a small simple cross on it. When it was held up, the wind would blow into it and it would look like a real animal.' Somewhere exists the original flag, made of skin, perhaps a thousand years old.

In the tiny muddy lanes came the smell of ojakhuri – fried pork and potatoes. We'd feasted on the same the previous night, alongside a group of walkers from Latvia, and by candlelight as the power had gone out again. The ojakhuri was served with a plate of fried cabbage dusted with Svan salt ('fried cabbage' sounds better in Svan, Richard quipped).

The following day we walked with Beka again, towards the Ushba glacier which sits close to the Georgia–Russia border. All around, the lower mountains looked as though someone had thrown a green velvet shawl over them. Walking through woodland, a herd of white ponies marked the spot where a hut had been built in a clearing and it was there that we met border guards who were eating strange rhubarb-like stalks, which they sprinkled Svan salt over, and shared with us. They were stationed there, they told us, more as a formality, than to diffuse actual threats but the very idea that Russian hikers would once have come over the mountains by foot made me think of another time, as did the old Russian pioneer camp we passed, now nothing more than foundations in the dirt.

Beka spoke of his love of climbing: 'there are many roads to Ushba, none of them easy.' He didn't walk with a trekking pole, but his elders might have used a möjra, a traditional wooden Svan walking stick with a metal tip.

Early in the season as it was, snow crevices and ice made it hard to go as far as we wanted but just being in the summertime mountains was reviving. That night, back at the hotel, it was the Georgian vegetable stew of adjapsandali for dinner, with freshly baked bread, and red wine from Kakheti tasting of blackcurrant and prune, again by candlelight which rather than an inconvenience, for us at least, added to the atmosphere. Afterwards, I went for a short walk from the hotel, up the lane, where in the distance small houses glowed with torches. It was peaceful, and very, very dark. To roughly echo the words of Georgian ethnographer Giorgi Chitaia: if you've never seen a mountain village on a moonlit night, then you've not seen Georgia.

We travelled back down from Svaneti in a shared marshrutka (minibus taxi), which despite careening at terrifying speed, took all day to reach Batumi on the Black Sea. As we bumped along, white-knuckled, I found myself pointlessly shifting my body weight to try and save us from sliding over the edge. And to distract thoughts of skidding off the road, I began casting my mind back to the previous summer when I'd had the good fortune of walking elsewhere in the mountains of Georgia.

# Adjapsandali – Georgian-style Ratatouille

Adjapsandali is a crowd-pleaser, one that is regularly on the menu in many Georgian cafés. This one isn't particularly authentic – dried marigold petals would be needed for that – but it is quick and easy, making it ideal for the family midweek table.

## SERVES 4

2 tbsp sunflower oil

1 small aubergine (eggplant), cut into bite-size pieces

Sea salt and freshly ground black pepper

2 large onions, roughly chopped

1 large chilli, deseeded and finely chopped

1 red or yellow bell pepper, roughly chopped

2 garlic cloves, grated

½ tsp cayenne pepper

½ tsp ground cumin

½ tsp dill seeds

1 large potato, chopped into bite-size pieces

260g/9¼oz canned peeled plum tomatoes

Handful of mixed fresh herbs, leaves and tender stems (basil, parsley, coriander (cilantro) and celery leaves all work well), chopped

Juice of ½ lemon

Heat 1 tablespoon of the oil over a high heat in a large, lidded casserole then stir-fry the aubergine with a good pinch of both salt and pepper until completely soft. Remove and set aside. Add the remaining tablespoon of oil, then the onions, chilli and bell pepper. Cook until nicely coloured, then add the garlic and spices, and cook for another couple of minutes. Add the potato, stir to coat it in the spices, then add the tomatoes and 100ml/scant ½ cup of water, bring to the boil and put the lid on to let it bubble for at least 15 minutes. Check the potato is cooked through, add the aubergine back in, then check the seasoning. Leave to bubble for 5 minutes more. When ready, stir through the fresh herbs and freshen with the lemon juice. Serve warm.

# THE MAGNETISM OF MOUNT KAZBEK

Part of the hypnotism of mountain peaks is that they seem both far away and close enough to touch. Reaching up above the earth, it is hard to imagine them rooted in the very same ground that we walk upon. For those reasons, mountains are also a route into daydreaming.

So as James and I went bumping down from Svaneti in the hair-raising minibus, pictures played out in my mind of the previous summer when I had gone with my friend Meagan Neal, world-class hiker and Executive Director of the Transcaucasian Trail (TCT) initiative, to walk around the snow-dusted Chaukhi massif, a huge thrust of sharp pinnacles that looks a little like the Italian Dolomites. When complete, the TCT will be a long-distance hiking route more than 3,000 kilometres in length, following the Greater and Lesser Caucasus Mountains and connecting roughly two dozen national parks and protected areas. It is a staggeringly brilliant effort and one that has at its heart the wish to transcend geopolitics and to bring people together in Georgia, Armenia and Azerbaijan.

It was an easy, sunny, alpine amble, with the added thrill of a small river crossing and a few thin snow bridges that we hopped over. Afterwards, we overnighted in Stepantsminda, a nearby touristy townlet, popular for its mountain views and surrounding valleys. It is chaotically overbuilt but does offer superb panoramas, the sort to make you silent with admiration. I sat on the guesthouse veranda watching the scenery turn the colour of candyfloss and I felt content not just because of the walk, and the view, but also because of the meal we'd shared.

It was at one of those small mountain places, not much bigger than a bunker, whose owners peel the vegetables, pour the drinks and smoke cigarettes, as well as waiting on customers. Few turn up just for the food, yet the café side is well done. Lentil soup, khinkali dumplings and bread, all served fresh and warm. Beneath our table, huge stiff-legged mountain dogs shifted at the aroma. It was a meal that was successful not only for its much-needed nutrients and rehydrating properties, but because it marked the end of a day well spent in the hills, in excellent company. And then there was the view, looking over my shoulder as we left, at dusk, it was there, unmistakable, Mount Kazbek: an extinct volcano also known as Mkinvartsveri, which roughly translates as 'ice mountain'.

In bed that night, mindful of the great mountain just beyond, which I could not see but could very much feel, my thoughts turned to myths and past explorers.

Mount Kazbek was in the sights of the British climber and author Douglas Freshfield, who we met earlier, and who wrote of it in *Travels in the Central Caucasus and Bashan*. The account includes an attempt to 'attack' the great mountain in summer, when he observed the ridges were 'up to their summits clothed in green'.

Many believe his team was the first to successfully summit the peak, but, again, who can really say? Georgians may well have preceded him. Freshfield was a grandiose figure (born into a family that had made a fortune in the East India Company, educated at Eton and Oxford and a lawyer by profession), and this comes through in his recollections and anecdotes. When enlisting a local climber, a celebrated hunter named Alexis, who had clearly elucidated his credentials for getting a team safely up Kazbek, Freshfield casually dismisses him as 'a feeble creature'. Eventually, Alexis was reluctantly hired due to a lack of anyone else forthcoming.

Freshfield was often scornful. On browsing bazaars in Tbilisi, he noted furriers selling animal skins. From Azerbaijan, there were orange and black furs from the now extinct Caspian tiger, from Bukhara there were curly karakul lambskins and from Georgia's own mountains there were thick bear pelts, all piled up next to pistols and guns. But despite such extravagant offerings he quickly concluded that the markets of Cairo and Tabriz did it better. Of Georgian wines from Kakheti, the region best known today for viticulture, he had little to say on the outstanding taste and terroir: 'very cheap, and is said to have the peculiar properties of curing gout and never causing headaches.'

### BROILED HAM AND A BREW OF MULLED WINE

One of Freshfield's primary aims in Georgia was the summit of Mount Kazbek, 'a magnificent mass of rock and snow', and in his book he recalls how its fame extended far beyond its slopes. He draws a lot from an Armenian he'd met called Khatissian, who'd made studies of Kazbek's nearby glaciers, and who told him that Ossetians, an ethnic group of the Caucasus, have been known to refer to the peak as Christ's Mountain. Freshfield also claimed that Khatissian told him fantastical tales about the peak. How once a band of monks lived in cells on the eastern flank, and that a saint dwelled among them whose holy book would levitate in a sunray that penetrated through a gap in the wall of the mountain. And how later a storm destroyed the cells forcing the hermits to flee. And, most bizarrely of all, that a crystal castle sits atop the summit holding a golden dove.

Freshfield also referred to another unnamed traveller for whom Kazbek was 'the very birthplace of magic' and where 'Medea compounded her love potions and poisons'.

This all sounds improbable but mysticism still intertwines freely with mountains today, whether by religious ecstasy, with mountains viewed as god's temples, or as places of limitless inspiration.

On 30th June 1868 Freshfield and his team began their ascent, helped by horses as far as they could go, heading to the 'snout of the Ortzviri glacier' on the southern side. Later, bivouacking in a mossy hollow at 3,400 metres, the group prepared an impressive mountain meal: 'excellent soup, broiled ham, and a brew of mulled wine'. Mulled wine! At 7p.m., they managed some sleep before setting out at 2.45a.m., shooting a pistol into the air to rouse the porters, who did not rise. Assuming their helpers 'had retired to lairs at some little distance, and out of sight', Freshfield went on with his friends, but without the missing guides, cutting steps into the ice, using ropes and axes to climb. By 11a.m. the group was exhausted and the wind was raging.

'It was just midday when we saw... the highest point of Kazbek was under our feet.' They stayed on the summit for ten minutes, unable to leave any memento, or cairn, to prove their climb, 'the rocks were too big to use for building a stone man'. With the ascent so treacherous, they descended the northern flank.

Between climbing Mount Kazbek and Mount Elbrus, Freshfield also remarked upon the celebrated natural springs of Georgia: 'Mineral springs abounded ... and coloured the ground for many yards round their source. An abominable stench ... probably arose from a sulphur spring.' His party puts this down to 'vegetation lying amongst the debris of the avalanches'.

It was to such sulphurous waters that Meagan and I briefly headed the following day.

# Transcaucasian Trail Mix

Having a pouch of trail mix in your pocket is always a good idea and it's easy to make up a bag of it, especially when you're in countries like Armenia and Georgia where bazaars are so generously filled with giant tubs of dried fruits and nuts. This version, with dried apricots and dates, has a hint of luxuriousness care of dark chocolate and a light dusting of aromatic nutmeg (the dates do make for a slightly sticky trail mix; if this is an issue best to leave them out). I also like to mix a handful of this through natural live yogurt and chopped banana for breakfast.

**MAKES 725G/1LB 9½OZ, ENOUGH FOR 1 LARGE JAR**

100g/3½oz hazelnuts, roughly chopped

75g/2½oz cashews, roughly chopped

75g/2½oz sunflower seeds

75g/2½oz pumpkin seeds

100g/3½oz dark chocolate

100g/3½oz dates, pitted

100g/3½oz dried apricots

100g/3½oz flame raisins

¼ tsp sea salt, crumbled

Pinch of grated nutmeg

Toast the nuts and seeds in a dry frying pan over a medium heat, stirring for 5 minutes. Allow to cool then chop the chocolate, dates and apricots into roughly pea-size pieces and combine with all the ingredients in a large bowl and mix well. Store in a sealable bag or airtight jar.

# RAMBLING THROUGH THE COLOURS OF TRUSO GORGE

After our stay in Stepantsminda, Meagan and I went tramping through Truso Gorge. And as we walked above the Terek River, eating trail mix and discussing the war in Ukraine, we marvelled at quivering irises, with their pointy deep-purple petals, that grew from the grassy trails we walked upon. Meagan led the way, through this ancient glacial valley stained blood-red, peach and ancient bronze from iron oxides, to the mineral spots she knew.

The gorge, not far from the Georgian Military Road which leads up to the Russian border and Mount Kazbek, has dozens of mineral springs, each one exuding salts, sulphur compounds and gases. A theatrical topography of water and rock. One lake, bubbling fiercely as a jacuzzi, was shrouded with a faint eggy smell sometimes associated with hot springs.

That summer, as we walked in Georgia's far north, a scandal had been making headlines involving Moscow, Tbilisi and Georgia's iconic mineral water, Borjomi. Factory workers at the forested spa town that gives the bottled water its name, located to the west of Tbilisi, had been busy striking.

Sold throughout the Russian Empire from the 1890s – the factory was photographed by Sergei Prokudin-Gorsky, a travelling photographer who documented the empire – Borjomi is still Georgia's best-known export, a source of national pride. Believed to help hangovers (though my personal research suggests that Likani, its sister brand, is more effective), Borjomi is relied upon to instantly cool bodies, with many people swearing by its health benefits.

## WATER WARS AND SANCTIONS

Part of the problem was that the company, IDS Borjomi, had, for some years, been majority-owned by an investment company run by the billionaire Russian-Israeli businessman Mikhail Fridman, and as he faced sanctions (by the UK, where he also lived) there were disruptions in export markets. Both Ukraine and Russia are, usually, top importers of the water. The company halted production, the workers went on strike and bottling was suspended. Some news outlets reported that the spring water was actually being poured away into the Gujaretistskali River.

Eventually, an agreement was drawn up between the Georgian government and Borjomi so that the majority-ownership was no longer Russian and which meant the company could avoid penalties. Essentially, the deal meant that Borjomi would be classed as Georgian allowing it to skip Western sanctions. Georgia was quick to deny that it was, in effect, helping Russian-owned businesses to operate.

Sometimes, the benefit of a walk is not only what you immediately see, but also the associations it brings, and what the scenery's physical arrangements make you think about. How walking mindfully can offer a bridge into other lives and places. Seeing the mineral water up close, as well as the orange-hued colours of the rocks and the mountains surrounding them, somehow made the recent mineral water news of greater interest.

During my time spent in Georgia, in 2022 and 2023, though I'd heard about Borjomi shortages, I never noticed empty shelves or refrigerators. But then my favourite mineral water in Georgia is Nabeghlavi, also named after its location, out to the west of Georgia, in Guria, shouldering the Black Sea. And it was there that I also walked into other uncommon landscapes and unanticipated life stories.

# Kazbek Cooler

Citrusy with a herby twist, I'd like to dedicate this cocktail to the amazing Transcaucasian Trail (TCT) crew. The TCT walking trail heads through some of the places mentioned in this book, including Vayots Dzor in Armenia and Svaneti in Georgia and it is an ongoing project (neighbouring Azerbaijan is also included and trails there are evolving nicely). If you are thinking of a hike in the South Caucasus, as well as utilising the excellent Hike Armenia app, and their helpful information centre in downtown Yerevan, the TCT should be your very first port of call.

As for this cocktail, it is effortless to prepare and without any hard-to-source ingredients. Just the thing after a hot day hiking in the hills.

**MAKES 2 COCKTAILS**

| | |
|---|---|
| 5 fresh basil leaves | 60ml/4 tbsp vodka |
| 5 fresh mint leaves | Soda water |
| 1 tbsp caster (superfine) sugar | Ice cubes |
| Juice of 1 lemon | |

In a jug, muddle the herbs with the sugar and lemon juice using the end of a rolling pin. Stir in the vodka, add soda water to taste (1 part vodka to 2 parts soda is a good ratio), then strain into glasses and add ice.

# Tarragon Panna Cotta

When I came down from the hills around Mount Kazbek, I went for a solo dinner at Salobie Bia in Tbilisi and ordered one of the finest salads I have ever eaten: fat pinkish tomatoes mixed with caper-like jonjoli, also known as pickled Colchis bladdernut, and purple basil, all dressed in intensely nutty Kakhetian sunflower oil. 'Divine' would not be too strong a word for that salad.

Afterwards, I plumped for a panna cotta dessert which matched it in deliciousness. With just the faintest scent of tarragon this is an elegant and easy pudding to prepare, ideal for dinner parties as you can make it ahead, leaving it to set overnight. Simply scale up the quantities to serve more.

**SERVES 2**

125ml/½ cup double (heavy) cream

125ml/½ cup whole milk

Leaves from a small bunch of tarragon
(reserve a few good ones to decorate)

1 gelatine leaf

Scant 1 tbsp caster (superfine) sugar

Put the cream, milk and 6 or so tarragon leaves in a medium saucepan and slowly bring to the boil for 5 minutes. Remove from the heat and set the pan aside to cool. Crush the tarragon leaves into the cream with the back of a wooden spoon to release more of their flavour.

Next, soak the gelatine in a bowl of cold water (any amount) until entirely softened. Have ready 2 x 150ml/5fl oz ramekins, or similar (small teacups work).

Stir the sugar into the pan, bring the cream back to a simmer to dissolve the sugar, then pass it through a sieve into a jug. Rid as much water as possible from the gelatine leaf, then stir it into the hot cream where it will magically dissolve into nothing. Pour the mixture into the ramekins and allow to cool completely, then chill in the refrigerator for 6 hours or overnight. Place a fresh tarragon leaf or two in the centre of each panna cotta when ready to serve.

# HILL SONGS AND DEADLY MOONSHINE

During the summer in Georgia with James, after we had travelled down from Svaneti, we headed for Guria in the west of the country, known for its tea fields and rare grape varieties, to stay at a winery and guesthouse named Menabde. Our room, at the top of an old wooden balconied house crowned with a terracotta tile roof, came with a daybed surrounded by climbing vines, ideal for dreaming on.

The Black Sea was nearby and the nighttime storms and crackling humidity proved its proximity. As I sat out, stars sparkling above in the navy blue sky, listening to thunder clapping, I pictured the Caspian too, much, much further away and I felt, for the first time, between the two seas though Tbilisi and Yerevan were both truer centrepoints.

After the stormy night had passed, along with a bottle of Chkhaveri wine, the vines often planted near the coast and traditionally trained to grow up trees, drained quickly and easily, we sat down to breakfast. The crusty morning rolls, served with a huge teapot of local black tea, had been scented in an ingenious fashion: each white roll had a little cinnamon stick poking out of its side like a pipe. Delicious with homemade citrus jams. But mainly breakfast was about Gurian khachapuri, an entirely new variation for us and one we both raved about for days afterwards. How is it different from khachapuri elsewhere in Georgia? Well, it was nothing to admire initially, though the top of the bread was nicely golden and lightly blistered, but on cutting it open the knife exposed perfectly quartered boiled eggs inside surrounded by supremely fluffy, slightly oniony, souffle-like cheese filling.

'Incredible, incredible. Cannot be beaten,' we mumbled between mouthfuls. It prompted that great Georgian word for which there is no English equivalent: shemomechama, which loosely translates as, 'I accidentally ate the whole thing.'

All that considered, the Black Sea storms, the neighbourhood tea, the distinctive wine, the exceptional khachapuri, we knew exactly where we were: Guria. And I cannot say the name of Georgia's tea-growing region without thinking of the all-male Rustavi Choir's classic song, 'Going to Guria', which, performed a capella, is surely one of the most beautifully haunting songs ever written. While Rustavi, with its celebrated choir, is located close to Tbilisi, it is Guria that is famous for its legendary singers.

Leaving the guesthouse behind we set off to walk, first passing the football pitch opposite where during the day large pigs nibbled the grass, keeping it neat and short, while from dusk onwards teams of boys took over to play on the field.

Muddy lanes led us to Shemokmedi village and our first stop: a tiny wooden house that once belonged to the folk singer Varlam Simonishvili, its roof topped with the same ochre tiles as the winery. Surrounded by flowering kiwi trees, the porch was reached by crossing a short bridge arched over a stream. There was no sign, and it looked much like the other neighbouring houses. We had called ahead the previous day and an elderly lady had answered explaining that while she was in mourning we would be welcome if we could return tomorrow. We said we were sorry to disturb her but she had insisted we should visit.

When we arrived, the lady we'd spoken to opened the door and ushered us onto the veranda, and then inside. Her name, she told us with a smile showing an immaculate set of teeth, was Nunu Goguadze.

We stepped into a spotlessly tidy wood-panelled room, its walls entirely covered with solemn but fantastic black and white portraits of the singer flanked by other important Gurian locals. There also stood a table with a modern framed photograph of a middle-aged man, looking directly at the camera, as in a passport photo, that had clearly been taken not so long ago. It sat next to a bowl of apples. The photograph, we learned, was of Nunu's son.

A rooster crowed outside and we were asked to sit. Then, immediately, motioning to the portrait, she told us what had happened. 'Eight months ago he died. He was 45 years old and he was poisoned from drinking something bad, cognac we think. Two people in the same drinking party died. They were friends celebrating the birth of a child.'

Shocked at the terrible news, we extended our sympathies. Nunu nodded and a deep sadness quickly seeped into the space. Disappearing for a few minutes, she returned with a pitcher of cherry kompot for us. Her family connection to the famous singer, she explained, is that Varlam Simonishvili was her husband's grandfather.

'Simonishvili was born in this house, lived all his life in this house and died in this house.' She lives here now, she explained, looking after things, but only in the warmer months. 'There are a few holes in the roof,' she added pointing up.

'I'm not here in the winter, it is too cold. But it is better to live here than in town, with clean air, harvesting tomatoes in the garden, all the fruits, and with good water. When I'm living in Ozurgeti [the main regional town], I feel heavy. I am 72 years old now but here, I get up early in the mornings, at six o'clock, and I feel sprightly.'

The portraits had been gathered together by the family from the old Soviet-built cultural house in the village. There were none of the more typical cabinet displays you find in similar house museums, holding songsheets, personal items, trinkets, costumes and trophies, in this one it was all about the pictures on the walls, and of simply being inside the house, of stepping into the atmosphere and the residues of brilliant talent. Simonishvili, long dead, did very much still occupy the space. Better, Nunu told us, to have the precious portraits here, a documentation of his life in a more fitting setting.

Stalin was a fan of his music and gave him a gold medal, she told us. 'He was very famous. If you mention his name in Tbilisi, or anywhere in Georgia, people know him. Once in a while I hear someone humming his songs. I never met him but my mother was in an ensemble and they sang the melodies though nobody is carrying on his songs just as he sung them nowadays,' Nunu lamented.

One of the quotes hanging on the wall, taken from his poems and songs, roughly translated as: 'Sing well, have a sweet voice.' He was very handsome when he was young, we all agreed, admiring the portraits. And with that she began to hum, pouring out more kompot. She wondered out loud if her grandson might take up the house museum one day.

All the room needed to complete it, I thought to myself, would be a gramophone playing the music. Looking around, I worried about the humidity seeping into the portraits.

'It is medicine for me, this house. But now let's see the garden,' Nunu said, standing up.

The garden, bursting forth with fruit, vegetables and herbs, felt a contrast. The stillness of the single-room museum, frustratingly impaired by a lack of funds and visitors (nobody had come for months we were told), versus the activity of Nunu's gardening. Clearly, this was a family of talent, of culture and Nunu had developed her daily ways and habits to cope with the tragic loss of her son, but there was also loneliness. As we parted, expressing our sincere thanks, I was left with questions, two of which were: what would happen to the museum when Nunu is no longer around to take care of it? And did she question why we came?

Leaving the house behind, we walked along a road lined with detached Gurian homes, almost all with a veranda, an impressive lawn or well-tended vegetable patches, for around 40 minutes before turning up a steep hill to Shemokmedi Monastery, past a graveyard. And there, among the tombs, we were met with beehives busy with industry. Their honey, sweetness and sound perhaps a gift, or company, for the dead. The monastery was set high above the Bzhuzhi River and from the top, where it was 30°C in the sun, lizards shot between rose bushes, gravestones and palm trees. Far in the distance, densely forested hills met the mountains of Adjara.

A priest with a kind face and the palest blue eyes imaginable appeared and began telling us, in Russian, a little of his life. He had been at the monastery for 19 years but when he was 20 he had worked as a sailor on Georgian Black Sea merchant ships. 'Look here, you see these marks on the wall? Those black marks? They are marks from hands. During Soviet times, when the church was closed, people would turn up anyway and run their thumbs across the outside wall.'

The monastery exuded auspicious energy, and the priest said proudly that Sunday services attract over four hundred people. It is an important place, with a 12th-century basilica, and a local queen buried in a white marble tomb inside, along with the bishops of Shemokmedi. A little later, the priest returned to us again holding two black and white photographs that had been taken in 1899 showing a gathering at the church of all the local bigwigs: holy men, intelligentsia in hats, and the police.

The same medieval monastery had captured the heart of London-born scholar and linguist Marjory Scott Wardrop, who is best remembered for making the first translation into English of the Georgian epic poem *The Man in the Panther's Skin*, written in the 12th century by Shota Rustaveli. A photograph of her in national Georgian dress, taken in 1896 by Georgia's first professional photographer, Alexander Roinishvili, is held at Weston Library, part of the Bodleian Library, in Oxford. Her journey to Georgia and her scholarship had been harder to secure than it was for her brother, British diplomat Sir Oliver Wardrop, who had studied the language and taken trips to the Caucasus. The Bodleian neatly summed up her challenges in the accompanying text of their exhibition Sappho to Suffrage, Women Who Dared: 'As a woman, she enjoyed no such opportunities and lamented this, as seen in this letter of 1894 to her brother: "I have got to stay home just doing nothing when I ought to be living, learning and working."' But she got there in the end, and made huge progress, teaching herself Georgian, then visiting the country and eventually becoming a trailblazer for promoting Georgian culture to the wider world.

In her copy of *The Man in the Panther's Skin*, the Bodleian Libraries note that she underlined a particularly telling section in the poem where the lion's cubs are equal, whether male or female. Her modesty is also highlighted in their biography of her: 'Wardrop refused to publish her translation during her lifetime, insisting it was not fit for publication. It was finally published in an edition prepared by her brother after her early death, and remains the standard against which other English translations of it are judged.'

While staying at the town of Ozurgeti, nowadays just a ten-minute drive away from Shemokmedi, the Wardrops were invited by the abbot to dine with him at the monastery. Back then, by carriage, it was a tough journey: 'We have good reason to remember this river, for our carriage was many times nearly overturned in rattling over its rocky bed, while the water was within about an inch of our feet.'

When they were due to leave, the townspeople gave them a stupendous farewell banquet: 'I shall never forget the enthusiasm and goodwill of these kind Gurians. Time after time they entreated us to come back soon, and we had countless invitations to country houses. The banquet lasted about two hours, and only came to an end because we were obliged to leave by the evening train for Batum [Batumi]. Among the eighty guests were some very tall men – three of them being about seven feet high. Before departing one of these drank a bottle of native champagne, without taking breath, to our happy journey. At last we drove off amid the cheers of all the assembled guests, who came out on the balcony to bid us good-bye.'

By the time we left the friendly priest and the monastery it was mid-afternoon. We'd walk to the tea plantation tomorrow. Guria had a way, we agreed, of slowing you down.

That night, back at the winery, we feasted again: chestnut soup with bacon, ajapsandali, tomato salad with walnuts, trout with walnut-based sauce. More of the supreme Chkhaveri wine, more of the superior Nabeghlavi mineral water. I will forever regret not trying the cornbread baked in cherry leaves. But that, at least, is one reason to return.

# Gurian Khachapuri

Not as visually striking as a boat-shaped Adjarian khachapuri, with its sunny egg shining in the centre, but this rustic khachapuri is profoundly delicious, and impressive, served warm for breakfast or brunch.

**MAKES 1 LARGE KHACHAPURI**

**FOR THE DOUGH**

200g/1½ cups minus 1 tbsp strong white bread flour, plus extra for dusting

7g/¼oz fast-action dried yeast

1 tsp fine sea salt

1 tsp caster (superfine) sugar

90g/scant ½ cup natural yogurt

1 egg, beaten, for glazing

**FOR THE FILLING**

1 spring onion (scallion), white and green parts, finely chopped

70g/2½oz mozzarella, chopped

60g/2¼oz feta, crumbled

60g/2¼oz ricotta

Sea salt flakes and freshly ground black pepper

1 large hard-boiled egg, peeled and quartered

1 tbsp extra-virgin olive oil

Put the flour into a large bowl, adding the yeast to one side and the salt and sugar to the other. Stir through the yogurt and add 5 tablespoons of lukewarm water. Mix to bring the dough together. Tip onto a lightly floured surface and knead until soft and silky, about 10 minutes (adding more flour as necessary). Form into a ball, place in a lightly oiled mixing bowl and cover with a damp tea towel. Leave to rise in a warm place for about an hour until roughly doubled in size.

When the dough is almost ready, line a baking sheet with parchment paper and preheat the oven to 200°C/400°F/gas mark 6.

Next make the filling. In a large bowl combine the spring onion with the cheeses, and mix well with ¼ teaspoon of black pepper and add just a pinch of salt.

Roll out the dough on a floured surface into a 35cm/14in disc. Put the filling in the middle and even out – you'll have a large gap around the edge and that is fine. Put the egg quarters evenly spaced onto the cheese filling. Drizzle with olive oil and dust with more black pepper. Using your finger wet the rim of the dough and bring up the edges as evenly as possible. Once you have a closed money bag shape, dust with flour and turn it over using both hands, so that the sealed side is underneath: be careful as it is heavy. Press down a few times, or gently roll a rolling pin over the surface without tearing the dough, until you have an unevenly shaped round of about 20cm/8in. Place on the lined baking sheet and brush with the beaten egg. Scatter over a few sea salt flakes. Bake until puffed up and golden, about 25 minutes. Leave to rest and cool, then slice and serve.

# BY FOOT ALONG GEORGIA'S TEA ROUTE

My introduction to Georgian tea came when I was researching *Black Sea* in northeastern Turkey. There, in the impossibly humid tea fields around Rize, I met Georgian seasonal workers who were in the fields picking tea leaves. I spotted the crucifixes on chains around their necks, wondered who they were, and then watched as after they'd finished work they jumped into the back of a truck, flopping down onto the tea sacks, and went by waving and singing in Georgian. Later, I learned about the legend of tea being carried from the Caucasus in a walking staff, to be grown in Turkey.

More recently, I was reminded of Georgian tea again in the famous Tbilisi tea shop run by Shota Bitadze and his son. The displays inside, museum-like and illuminating, included photographic prints of tea workers taken by Sergei Prokudin-Gorsky, the tsar's colour photographer.

As an early adopter of colour photography Prokudin-Gorsky visited the Caucasus first in 1905 to chronicle people, infrastructure, factories, farms and rural communities. Travelling through Georgia he photographed the Borjomi water factory, the streets of Tbilisi (then known as Tiflis), palm trees around the Black Sea coast, Batumi, and bamboo forests there which, given their unlikeliness to thrive elsewhere in the Russian Empire, would have appeared unimaginably exotic.

And he took the portraits of tea workers, copies of which are displayed in the little tea museum-shop in Tbilisi today. One in particular stood out to me: a portrait of Lao Jin Jao, who, born in China, was captured by Prokudin-Gorsky standing on his Georgian tea plantation, wearing black galoshes, wide yellow trousers, a blue Mandarin collar vest and black hat. The date it was taken is vague, between 1905 and 1915, but what is known is that by the time of the photo, Lao Jin Jao had won a prestigious gold medal at the Paris Exposition in 1900 for his tea grown on Georgia's Black Sea coast, a venture that had only been going for roughly fifty years.

On the topic of the world's favourite hot drink, I had been told by today's tea experts working in Georgia that the Megreladze family in Guria would fill me in on the historic details and how crisis after crisis brought this enterprising industry to its knees.

The walk to reach Lika Megreladze's tea project was slow and hot. From Menabde, the winery where we were staying, we tramped along roads bordered by wattle fences for five kilometres or so following signs advertising the 'tea route', a fledgling agro-tourism initiative with an aim to bring tourists into the green hills of Guria.

Lika greeted us in perfect English and led us into her traditional wooden house, which was, she explained, rebuilt by her great-grandfather, a farmer, in 1907. Every structural detail in the room had been made by hand and was original. Outside, bugs and beetles buzzed around wicker baskets of tea tips already picked from the small tea plantation. A Ukrainian flag flapped in the breeze next to an EU one. A message to visiting Russians, Lika explained, of her unwavering support for Ukraine.

After we'd sat down, having admired the extraordinarily broad Georgian tea-picker hats, we began with Lao Jin Jao and how he came to kickstart global interest in Georgian tea.

Frustrated with China leading global tea production, Russia looked to develop its own industry. Exploratory tea plantation projects into the empire's warmer corners included Georgia and the first was developed around 1847. Knowing experts were needed for this delicate crop, a team of Chinese tea growers, led by agriculturist Lao Jin Jao, were brought in during the late 19th century to oversee production. A tea grower's base, a grand house complete with a distinctive turret, was built not far from the Black Sea city of Batumi, in a small town named Chavki.

The *Iveria* newspaper of the time backed this up, claiming that in the winter of 1893 a ship arrived bringing ten thousand tea plants to Batumi, along with several Chinese tea workers. The same newspaper, in summer 1897, reported: 'Twenty-eight men, bringing 700 poods [a pood was roughly 16 kilos] of tea seeds, arrived in Chavki a few days ago … [and] tea growers well known in China came with them to oversee the cultivation process.'

It was a productive time for western Georgia. Batumi had become a free port in the late 19th century, encouraging the opening of factories and plants, and in 1876, the Swedish industrialists, Ludvig and Robert Nobel (brothers of Alfred Nobel, founder of the Nobel Prizes), arrived looking for wood suitable for arms production and instead found a different opportunity, an oil industry in its infancy. By 1883 they had founded the Batumi Oil Terminal.

While the Chinese focused on tea culture, Turks pushed the tobacco industry, and as a result of such newly found wealth splendid villas were built, sea bathing became fashionable and manicured gardens began to line Batumi's seafront. Then, in 1900, came the construction of the Baku–Tbilisi oil pipeline, marking another new era. This was followed, shortly after, in 1907, by the wine company Daniela & Co known for producing and exporting Georgian wine that had been bottled in Batumi.

But the Bolshevik Revolution of 1917, which sent the photographer Prokudin-Gorsky fleeing to Paris, saw many, though not all, tea bushes destroyed to make way for food crops. Georgia's tea enterprise was now in peril from a widespread desire to mechanise, economise and collectivise.

Lika sipped her tea and continued with her own story. 'In the Soviet period, when I grew up, there were only tea plantations here, and they belonged to the kolkhoz [collective farm]. You walked in the lanes and tea was all you could smell. My mother who is now 85 years old, worked at the Anaseuli tea institute, with its own microclimate, which was a centre for subtropical culture, though now it is a bit abandoned.'

Pulling out black and white photographs she'd collected from her neighbours, she also showed us beautiful old tea tins with carpet-like designs, and colour magazines from the 1980s with tea pickers as cover stars, one showing the Soviet geneticist Kseniya Bakhtadze on a tea plantation in Georgia, her lapels covered with medals.

'By 1925, "Gruzinski chai" [Georgian tea] was marketed as something the Soviets had made first. Keen to expand, Soviet leaders even tried planting tea in Crimea, where they thought it would grow but it was too dry there. Guria however with its Black Sea humidity is perfect for tea.'

The Soviets wanted their own tea but as with everything from baking to milking to textiles, what was previously small scale and carefully done in villages from Kazakhstan to Ukraine and everywhere in between, was quickly mechanised for maximum production, to serve the enormous Soviet Union. Soon, there were tea plantations and tea factories not just in Guria but elsewhere in Georgia, such as the regions of Samegrelo and Imereti. Workers were bussed around the country and Georgia grew to be one the world's largest producers of tea. At one point, more than a million plants were taken every year to Turkey. It was a huge enterprise not just in terms of growing but of equipment and machinery – everything that goes into the process.

But the industry collapsed, along with the Soviet Union, in 1991, and that same year Georgia slid into a severe crisis with a vicious war that saw the central streets of Tbilisi booming with artillery and tanks rolling towards the parliament. Things were so hard that in the early 1990s material from the tea factories was sold as scrap metal. A few families, such as Lika's, became keepers of traditional Georgian tea making, holding the clues that could one day revive it back to life.

'What if the Soviets had not come, if tea had never become industrial?' I asked. After all, tea, not from tea plants but rather from mint, thyme and mulberry leaves, had been drunk by Georgian highlanders for centuries.

'It would be great, the tea would have been the very best quality,' Lika answered. 'Georgian tea was so good but Soviet planners drove up production and ruined its reputation. But now it's coming back.'

After 35 years in Tbilisi, Lika is happy to be in Guria, where she also makes wine, around 800 bottles a year. 'I only roll a little tea, it is more for experience and to show how it is done.' Her role is more educator and storyteller than producer. Buying a bottle of wine, and a pouch of the precious tea, we each put on a ginormous tea-picker's hat to walk down to the bushes, and onwards to a stream and a bamboo thicket.

It was an idyllic setting, and an interesting story, but I had started to itch. I wanted to see what remained of Lao Jin Jao's tea headquarters, whatever state it may be in, right on the Black Sea.

# Chestnut and Bacon Soup

Inspired by the velvety soup served at the excellent Menabde winery guesthouse in Guria, this is precisely the sort of hydrating and hearty dish that comforts body and mind after a long walk.

**SERVES 4**

2 tbsp olive oil

2 rashers smoked streaky bacon, rinds removed and chopped very small

180g/6¼oz cooked and peeled whole chestnuts

1 celery stick, chopped

1 small onion, chopped

1 small carrot, peeled and chopped

1 litre/4⅓ cups vegetable stock

Sea salt and freshly ground black pepper

Heat 1 tablespoon of the oil in a frying pan and fry the bacon pieces until crisp and well coloured. Remove a third or so of the pieces and set aside.

Add the remaining tablespoon of oil to a large, lidded saucepan or casserole, add the fried bacon from the frying pan and all the other ingredients except the stock. Season with salt and pepper, and stir-fry for 5 minutes over a medium heat, then add the stock, put the lid on and simmer very gently for 45 minutes.

Once the soup is ready, allow it to cool slightly, then blitz with a stick blender, and check the seasoning. Ladle into bowls and top with the reserved bacon.

# PROMENADING THE BLACK SEA'S GREEN CAPE

After the Nobel prize-winning novelist John Steinbeck had completed his 40-day trip to the Soviet Union in 1947, along with the photographer Robert Capa, he published a book called *A Russian Journal*. In that book, he points out how Russians collectively fetishized Georgia and its people. How they viewed Georgians as the best drinkers, lovers, musicians and dancers. And not only that, how they saw Georgian land as not only a dream vacation destination but an actual living paradise that they'd choose over heaven for their afterlife, somewhere with nice air and 'its own little ocean', meaning the Black Sea.

But if you read *A Russian Journal* you'll notice how Steinbeck, eating indulgently but failing at shots of chacha, 'a veritable rocket of a drink', quickly began to roll out the very same stereotypes himself. Georgians, he noted, could out-drink them, out-eat them and had 'the fierce gaiety of the Italians' paired with an energy that 'not only survives but fattens on a tropical climate'. Everything they did, he concluded, was 'done with flair'.

Steinbeck toured the Black Sea coast of Georgia with Capa, seeing the orange groves and visiting the state-run tea farms. And, he noted with interest, it was women with clever fingers who not only did the tea picking but tended to the ovens and did the grading and packing as well. Even the director was a woman.

'It is a magical place, Georgia, and it becomes dream-like the moment you have left it,' Steinbeck mused as he departed, flying over the Black Sea, with a bag of peaches he wanted to carry to Moscow but which failed to ripen.

A slow train had taken this pair to Batumi, where they had arrived exhausted from weeks of navigating Soviet life. Batumi, long a holiday resort as much as an important Black Sea city, is not a bad place to recuperate, though, as I too, discovered 75 years after they had come, and ten years on from my first visit.

Palm-fringed, and laid out by Prussian gardeners in 1881, Batumi's boulevard heaved with holidaymakers and hundreds of Russian speakers for its entire length. It was unsettling to watch paragliders and children splashing in the water with the knowledge that just across the Black Sea a cruel war raged on, fought between invaders and those who've been invaded.

The very same nationalities sat on the sand and benches, selling one another drinks, lighting one another's cigarettes and speaking to one another, usually in Russian: Belarussians who'd fled (the government of Belarus has supported Russia's invasion), Russians from all across their giant land, and Ukrainians some of whom were also Russian speakers. There may be laws in place requiring businesses in Georgia to serve customers in the Georgian language, but it is Russian that is most commonly heard in certain places in Batumi, including the seaside.

Every night, just before dusk, a group of Ukrainians would stand in a neat line, in the very heart of the city, by the statue of Medea holding the golden fleece, and they would sing in Ukrainian. Their aim was, I felt, to come together, and to sing beautifully, in defiance, as much as it was to collect donations for the war effort back home.

The war was present in Batumi, but also not. It was summer, and there was a carefree attitude in the centre of town. Cafés did a roaring trade, and at night the bars stayed open until late. Georgian taxi drivers in Batumi would often speak of sailing the Black Sea. I met one who was soon to qualify as a sailor, another who'd retired, and one who had been training in Mariupol, Ukraine, on the Sea of Azov, but now the war had stalled his progress.

### ANCIENT COLCHIS FORESTS OF THE CAUCASUS

Salt-whipped and humid, the boulevard still was a good place to walk and read, and I was drawn to it most days. In the morning, and at dusk, sometimes running along it, too, a little thrilled at the prospect of jogging along the Black Sea coast, a body of water that has occupied my thoughts for well over a decade. But there is one other walk in Batumi that can easily rival the popular esplanade.

The Botanical Garden, spread over a hundred hectares and directly overlooking the Black Sea, is, quite simply, stunningly beautiful. It was one of the largest in the Soviet Union, and for any gardener, or hobby botanist, it is a living paradise and a garden you can happily get lost in. Looking out, the sea line touches the sky, melding the two together and giving rise to the sounds, if you know them, of Gershwin's 'Rhapsody in Blue'. Look to the left and you can see the outlandish architecture of Batumi, look straight ahead and you may see a tanker, look just below and you can see palm trees and a sea of green. From that vantage point in summer, it was the bluest Black Sea I had ever seen anywhere, not grey and brooding but tropical-looking and turquoise. Like the Andaman Sea. The trails through the garden are marked but they are also slightly confusing, so a walk demands that you go with the flow, which is the only way to stroll in such humidity. Sloping up and down, the pathways reveal greenhouses, little nooks and benches, one after the next.

And the garden also offers the chance to walk among the trees of the ancient Colchis forests of the Caucasus. There is *Picea orientalis* (Caucasus), *Pinus pallasiana* (Crimea), *Pinus pithyusa* (western Transcaucasus). IUCN Red List trees, and rare plants of the 'Trans-Caucasian Humid Subtropics' and vulnerable species including *Quercus pontica* from the subalpine mountains of western Georgia, *Betula medwediewii Regel* of the southern Colchis, *Buxus colchica* from the Georgian forest belt. The beautiful but endangered flowering *Salix kikodseae*, also Colchis, was hidden down a steep muddy path, entirely deserted.

This is a highly verdant section of the Black Sea, mellow and tepid. All that isn't built over with concrete has the chance to produce something useful and miraculous, such as eucalyptus, palms, bamboo, tobacco or cork trees. There are mulberries, which flourish almost everywhere in Georgia and whose cocooneries once provided silk for the USSR's parachutes and paratroops. Walnut trees, too. And the tung tree, introduced from China in the 1930s, which provided oil good for varnishing ships, essential for Black Sea trade.

If I'd never been to Georgia, I would come here, to the Botanical Garden in Batumi, first. To walk above the sea, to hear the train whistle coming from tracks far below taking passengers to Tbilisi, and to relish the warm salty breeze.

## AN ABANDONED TEA HOUSE ON THE BLACK SEA

If Tbilisi was tense, Batumi was less so, at least on the surface. Strikingly, anti-Russian graffiti was almost non-existent in the centre. But port cities have always been different. Traditionally cosmopolitan, and swollen on the sort of fast cash that comes with trade, they are used to turning a blind eye. The region also has a different history to the rest of Georgia. Until 1878 it was part of the Ottoman Empire and after the Ottomans ceded Adjara to the Russian Empire, Batumi gained a significant Russian-speaking population. On one street, I noticed that there wasn't a single Georgian number plate on any of the cars parked; most were Russian, a few were Ukrainian. Money was rolling in and every spare apartment was taken up by the newly arrived. But that isn't to say that hostility and fear weren't there as of course they were. There were protests after I'd left, in July 2023, when the *Astoria Grande* cruise ship was forced to leave after arriving in Batumi from the Russian port of Sochi. Protests broke out after some Russian tourists on the ship told local media that they supported Russia's 2008 war against Georgia.

One night, we returned to the popular long-standing restaurant, Fanfan, which we'd dined at back in 2013 during our first overland Black Sea journey, starting in London and ending in Tbilisi. Back then, Batumi was a different

place, seedier, stranger and attracting large numbers of gamblers and small-time businessmen. There was not the range of dining options that you find today. Fanfan was a safe bet. On going back, I worried it wouldn't be the same, and if it wasn't, that it would tarnish my memories. But I needn't have fretted. Housed in a building completed in 1905 and once owned by the Georgian writer and Soviet-era dissident Chabua Amirejibi, who spent fifteen years behind bars and was twice nominated for the Nobel Prize in literature, it had barely changed. Dahlias sat on every table just as I remembered. Mussels in blue cheese sauce remained on the menu. And I even recognised certain posters and lampshades. I ordered a bottle of white unfiltered Rkatsiteli from the Kakheti region which, tasting of apples and apricots, was the colour of peach when poured out. The label described it as 'the eternity of the sun living in a bottle', the sort of confidence that can only come from a winemaker following their own national method of winemaking that goes back thousands of years.

After a successful meal we returned to a small bar on a side street, close to the Christ the Saviour Armenian Apostolic Church, once used by the Soviets as a planetarium, and today fronted by a magnificent magnolia tree. The bar was an unpretentious spot, at odds with the swathe of Russian-run cafés selling overpriced coffee that surrounded it.

It was where James and I would have a drink most nights. We got to know the owner, a friendly woman originally from Gori, which was where, she told us, her father had been killed by Russians during the 2008 war. As we'd always order beer I'd never paid any attention to the cocktail menu on the wall. But then one night I saw it. 'White Russian' had been crossed out and chalked in its place a cocktail with a different name: 'Dead Russian'. We asked if it had caused any problems. 'I don't care if Russians don't like it. This is my bar,' she replied plainly.

Before leaving Batumi I fulfilled my promise to myself to see Lao Jin Jao's old tea headquarters in Chavki, not knowing what to expect. It still stood, but only just. Heavily graffitied and covered with tropical vegetation, it had not been entirely forgotten, though, as in blue paint someone had written on one side of the building, in English, Black Sea Tea.

The handsome green turret, like a pointy witch's hat, remained and most thrillingly of all inside there was an original mural of a tea leaf on the floor. And through one of the long-gone windows was a picture-perfect view of the Black Sea, the waves just a couple of metres away. If any building in the world deserved to be carefully rebuilt and turned into a working tea shop and café, it was this. One day, I'm sure, someone will find the funds to do it.

# Lobiani – Buttery Bean Bread

Everyone loves khachapuri but if you are in Georgia for a while you may not want to eat heavily cheese-laden bread all the time. Lobiani is lighter, filled with beans, great fuel for walking, and for those reasons it is by far my favourite stuffed Georgian bread. This is an unorthodox method that will get you something pretty close to the real thing, but made at home. Note: you'll need to soak the kidney beans overnight.

**MAKES 2**

**FOR THE DOUGH**

180g/1⅓ cups plain (all-purpose) flour, plus extra for dusting

7g/¼oz fast-action dried yeast

½ tsp salt

¼ tsp caster (superfine) sugar

1 large egg

1 tbsp sunflower oil, plus an extra drizzle

**FOR THE FILLING**

200g/7oz dried kidney beans

30g/2 tbsp butter

1 onion, very finely chopped or grated

1 tbsp Svan salt (or make a spice blend of 1 tablespoon, combining ¼ tsp salt, then a mixture of ground coriander seeds, blue fenugreek, dried marigold petals, garlic powder, red pepper flakes and caraway seeds; if you don't have all of these, use those you do have, but don't forgo the salt, which should be a quarter of the whole)

Soak your beans in the refrigerator overnight, drain and rinse in the morning. Put the beans in a saucepan and cover with fresh cold water. Bring to the boil and boil briskly for 10 minutes, reduce the heat and simmer until the beans are soft (about 35 minutes). Set aside, leaving the lid on to let them steam and cook further.

Sift the flour into a bowl, adding the yeast on one side and the salt and sugar on the other. Make a well in the middle, crack the egg into it, stir in the oil and 3 tablespoons of warm water while you mix with your other hand. Turn out onto a floured surface and knead for about 10 minutes, until soft. Return to the bowl, cover with a damp tea towel and place in a warm spot until the dough has doubled in size, about 1–1½ hours.

For the filling, add a pinch of salt and a drizzle of oil to the cooked beans, and using a potato masher, set to work mashing the beans as best you can, in the saucepan – they are quite stiff but they will cook down further in the next step so don't worry too much. Once mashed, warm a large frying pan over a medium heat and melt the butter. Add the onion and cook until soft and glossy, then stir in the Svan salt or your spice mix, cook until fragrant, 2–3 minutes. Add the beans, season really well with black pepper, and stir combining it all well, turn up the heat to high and add 2½ tablespoons of water. Stir, mashing with the spoon, until you have a thick smoothish consistency. Remove from heat and allow to cool.

Preheat the oven to 240°C/475°F/gas mark 9. Line 2 baking trays with parchment paper.

Once the bean mix is cool, punch down the dough and turn out onto a lightly floured surface, divide it into two, keeping the half you aren't working with covered with the tea towel to prevent it drying out. Roll out to a 25cm/10in round, and spoon half the filling in the centre of the dough circle, leaving a generous rim of 8cm/3¼in or so on all sides. Fold in the dough to cover the beans, then turn over seal side down, and gently run a rolling pin over the dough to even it out so you have a 20cm/8in filled flatbread. Cut a small cross in the middle to let the steam out. Repeat with the second dough half and the remaining filling. Slide the lobiani, sealed side down, onto the lined trays.

Bake for 20–25 minutes until golden and crisp. Cut into slices and serve warm. (Wrapped, they'll keep for a day or so and can be reheated.)

# Lobio Croquettes

These croquettes, ordered on a whim and eaten in a small restaurant in Batumi, were an unexpected smash hit. They really do need the sour tomato sauce, so don't skip that.

**SERVES 2**

2 tbsp sunflower oil

2 garlic cloves, crushed

½ tsp dried mint

½ tsp dried thyme

½ tsp dried oregano

240g/8½oz canned kidney beans, drained

1 tbsp red wine vinegar

1½ tbsp tomato purée (paste)

¼ tsp salt

¼ tsp freshly ground black pepper

40g/1½oz grated parmesan

**FOR THE COATING**

1 egg

35g/¼ cup plain (all-purpose) flour

1½ tsp paprika

35g/½ cup dried breadcrumbs

**To serve**

220ml/1 cup passata

1 tbsp lemon juice

Pink pickled onions or raw red onions, thinly sliced (optional)

Handful of watercress (optional)

Mayonnaise, for dipping

Heat the oil in a large frying pan, add the garlic and stir-fry until its pungency lessens then add the dry herbs. Cook over a low heat for 1 minute then add the drained beans, vinegar, tomato purée, salt and pepper, and turn up the heat to medium-high, cooking until any liquid has evaporated. Remove the pan from the heat and, once cooled, mash the beans and mix through the grated parmesan. It will be quite stiff and that's fine.

Using your hands, form the paste into oblong balls about 5cm/2in long – you should get about 8–10. Put on a plate and chill in the refrigerator for 30 minutes or so to firm up.

Line a baking tray with foil and preheat the oven to 180°C/350°F/gas mark 4.

Take three bowls. In the first, beat the egg, in the second put the flour and in the third mix the paprika through the breadcrumbs. Roll each croquette first in the flour, then the egg and finally, the breadcrumbs. Coat well on all sides.

Transfer the croquettes to the tray and bake for 20–25 minutes until golden and crisp.

To serve, warm the passata in a saucepan, season and sharpen with the lemon juice. Then pour a swirl of the passata onto 2 dinner plates to form a disc, put the croquettes on top, and, if you wish, crown them with slices of onions, either pickled or raw, and put some watercress on the side. They are good just like this but also benefit from being dipped into a wee pot of mayonnaise.

# WALKING FROM MOSQUE
# TO MONASTERY

Set back from Batumi's leafy boulevard is the Khariton Akhvlediani Adjara State Museum. And inside, surrounded by cabinet displays of dried tangerines, tea and tobacco, clues as to what thrives in the humid Black Sea climate, is a small wooden door propped against a wall. Like many museum items, whose futures are being debated around the world, it ought to be elsewhere, in this case the village of Akho, 65 kilometres east of Batumi's seafront. It was there that worshippers once used the door to enter the oldest-known mosque in Georgia's Adjara region, completed in 1818. The door I stood in awe of is the real thing, while the mosque in Akho, built during Ottoman rule, has had to make do with a replica. During the Soviet period, when churches became secular schools and mosques were reassigned as storage rooms, museum officials took the original door away and when the villagers of Akho appealed for its return they were denied and instead given a copy.

It is easy to see why the door is a museum piece. It is exquisite. Rich with intricate geometric patterns, it is similar to the columns and pillars around it, collected from surrounding villages, which when displayed together present a ligneous formation of symmetrical patterns carved into beech, chestnut and walnut: an Ottoman-style tulip here; a borjgali, symbol of the sun with rotating wings, there.

The craftsmen of the door were most likely Laz, traditionally inhabitants of the far eastern end of the Black Sea coast who have been long known as master carpenters, as the museum signage attests, describing them as 'perfect ornament makers'. The 18th-century Georgian prince, geographer and cartographer Vakhushti Bagrationi recognised their woodworking skills, stating that the Laz were 'men experienced in wood treatment and construction of boats' which they would use to travel between the ports of Batumi, Poti and Trabzon. In *Black Sea*, I wrote a little of their traditions and included a recipe for custard-filled Laz börek.

So alluring was the door that James and I set off in a hired car, aiming to see such woodwork in situ, encouraged by a guide of sorts that I'd been given to help us get there. My friend Meagan Neal had introduced me to a remarkable website and research project called Indigenous Outsiders which catalogues the endangered architectural legacy of village mosques in Adjara based on location, design and conservation. More than fifty such mosques, built between 1818 and 1926, survive today and they are mapped. Walking between them would take weeks so the best way was to drive, and to do a few shorter strolls.

Leaving Batumi behind, we were soon into the cool green hills where occasionally an enormous lone mansion would appear on the jade-coloured slopes. Closer to the roadside were gardens filled with pink damask roses, rugs airing, and granaries on stilts for keeping corn. It was impossible not to draw up memories of northeastern Turkey, especially the konaks (mansions) high above Çamlıhemsin and the green tea bushes dotted around in the misty province of Rize on the Black Sea.

Climbing steeply up a very narrow lane, our too-big saloon car perilously close to the edge, we reached the village of Zundaga (population: 300) with its sprawling manors fronted by semi-circular steps, and facades formed of smooth stones framed by timber, again, similar to those across the border in Turkey. All was deserted except for the tiny school and a teacher, standing at the entrance, had watched us drive in. Stopping, we explained the reason for our visit, in Russian, our only shared language. We were invited into the classroom. Three of just ten children registered were present. 'Hello!' they sweetly chanted in English.

'The key for the mosque is hidden under the mat, you're welcome to visit,' the teacher told us. But of course we couldn't find the key. It took a local farmer, dressed in galoshes and a saggy knitted vest, who we'd bumped into on a lane, to locate it under a wax tablecloth next to the stove in the vestibule. It was clear that half the fun of this expedition was going to be gaining access.

I let out a small gasp as we stepped inside. Built in the 1860s, it had been decorated by craftsmen, named in the trusty catalogue, handily accessible on my phone, as 'Usta Kabaz Ahmed (Laz) with locals Kajaia, Gogitidze, and Turmanidze', who'd combined wildly detailed floral motifs and interlocking meander patterns for the mihrab, minbar and mezzanine railings. Unpainted, and without lacquer, it had clearly been recently restored. We learned that in the cellar below, which operated as a barbershop under the Soviets, existed an active woodworking studio where the repairs took place. It felt a truly positive start to the tour.

**CANDY CANES AND CORNSTALKS**

Thanking the villagers, we turned back following tracks lined entirely by vivid blue hydrangeas, aiming for Uchkhiti (population: 260), the next village mosque on the map, a half-hour drive southwards. Lonely and lacking a minaret, we found it easily, but it was firmly closed. A shy local shepherd appeared as we hovered by a mulberry tree but all communication failed. On the doorstep sat an ancient pair of bathing clogs, dotted with termite holes, but there was little sign of life otherwise. The wooden exterior was reason enough to visit, though, elegant in its simplicity, untainted by plastic windows and spray foam insulation or corrugated metal cladding that we'd see at other mosques.

Undefeated, we carried on to hard-to-say Bzubzu (population: 306), to see one of the oldest mosques, constructed in 1820. Parking the car, we immediately drew attention from a small football pitch lively with school children, and soon enough a villager offered to lead the way to the mosque, which, painted cream and mustard, was surrounded by a peculiar range of mossy rocks protruding from the ground like giant camel humps. A teapot and a well-worn rug marked the entrance but inside, while it had been painted in different shades of blue, ir otherwise had very little ornamentation. I referred to the catalogue: plain maybe, but it is the only remaining mosque that had featured in a Soviet survey conducted by folk-art historians in the late 1950s: 'drawings of Bzubzu depict well-preserved Ottoman era decorative elements despite the passing of a century or more of time: a ceiling medallion framed by twining tulips and vines, a door covered entirely with intricate geometric patterns ... The contrast between Bzubzu in 1959 and its condition today is striking – little, if anything, remains of the ornaments so carefully documented by Soviet historians.'

While today's interior had nothing calling for applause, the liveliness of the football-playing village children gave it hope somehow. But the reality is that these distinctive mosques are in peril, which is why the Indigenous Outsiders project exists. I asked Angela Wheeler, a key contributor to the catalogue, about the challenges around both mindset and preservation. She told me:

'The mainstream view is that Islamic architecture in Georgia is a foreign element. It's Ottoman architecture that happens to be in Georgia. Soviet authorities took an almost opposite approach. Their primary concern was suppressing all local religions, Islam and Orthodoxy alike, so their solution was to focus on how these mosques were so aesthetically unusual that they didn't represent Islam at all: instead, they were examples of Georgian peasant folk art. It's Georgian art that happens to be in a mosque. These extreme political approaches miss the more complex truth of Adjaran mosques (and their communities), which is that they are fully Islamic and fully Georgian at the same time.'

We travelled on, heading to the village of Chao, where we would overnight, following the Adjaristskali River, a tributary of the Çoruh which rises in Turkey's Mescit Mountains. Then, rounding a corner, we were flagged down with a sign reading: 'Stop!' A landslide had occurred up ahead but so common are they that the way was cleared in under an hour. We continued, past the medieval Makhuntseti bridge, built of volcanic rock and limestone and in a characteristically high semicircle, because of frequent floods.

In Chao, we headed for the mosque, built in 1909. Beyond its protective shell of corrugated metal it was deeply artistic, with rustic cornstalks painted on the walls, lacy latticed balconies, and prayer rugs covering every inch of the floor. Almost everything was in soft pastel colours. A pink ribbon design stretched up the white pillars giving the appearance of candy cane; the dome, made by Laz craftsmen, was plain but lacquered and its arched ribs stood out all the more for its comparative modesty. Altogether, the drawings and colours reminded me of the folk art of Ukraine, or the painted rural houses of Poland. Chao itself, close to the ancient Furtio bridge, built in the 10th century for caravan routes, is facing its own ongoing struggle – continued depopulation due to a devastating landslide thirty-five years ago. It was easy to tour the mosques in a car but the following day we wanted to walk.

## THE GREEN, GREEN MOUNTAINS OF ADJARA

The next morning, as dawn filtered through the valley, we left Chao and started out from the regional capital of Khulo, a sleepy town famous for its verdant hills, and also its cable car. Perhaps primarily the cable car. This is a single cabin, connecting Khulo with the tiny village of Tago (population: 294), one and a half kilometres across the valley. It's the second longest pylon-free cable car in Europe and was built during the Soviet Union in 1985. And it was here, just before we stepped into the shiny red pod, that geopolitics came to the fore.

The only other passengers were two Russian men. They seemed a throwback, wearing tracksuits complete with leather man bags. Smoking cigarettes, they chatted and joked with the Georgian staff as we waited for the cable car. But when they realised that we were British, they didn't hesitate.

'Slava Ukraini', they both shouted the Ukrainian national salute in unison. And they meant it. They bounded over to shake our hands.

Ivan and Andrei were Russian businessmen from Nizhny Novgorod, they told us, and were here on holiday. It was a relief, they said, to be able to talk freely about their disgust at the Kremlin's invasion of Ukraine because back home, they couldn't. Despite the propaganda and threats, some people in Russia still hate their leader's 'special military operation' and this pair were indulging the fact that they were able to speak their mind on a Soviet cable car in Georgia.

An interesting start to the walk, I thought, as the slightly dicey-looking cable car wobbled us across the emerald-green valley, towards Tago. From there, the plan was to walk to Skhalta Monastery.

We disembarked into a field alive with wildflowers: yellow rattle, purple bellflower and whole banks of daisies typical of summer. A tall minaret marked the mosque that had been used as an agricultural warehouse under the Soviets. Inside, much of the original decoration had been lost and the dome was unpainted, though the ablution area was brightened by a striking blue and red floral rug.

Leaving Tago, past neat rows of vegetables, we walked into forests of walnut trees and past cows adorned with blue beaded necklaces (bringing to mind the decorated cattle of northeastern Turkey). The sky grew black, as though another storm was blowing in, and we lost time confused by a sign that was pointing in the wrong direction. We tramped on through wooded glens until, about eight kilometres later, we hit a road that first led to an agricultural cooperative, specialising in Chandler walnuts. Walnuts are so central to Georgian cookery, not a mere snack to be nibbled or to top a cake as is often the case in Britain, but rather an ingredient to be heavily called upon. There is the classic appetiser pkhali, vegetables pummelled with walnuts, garlic, and spices; walnut-heavy bazhe sauce, which goes so well with roast chicken; and the excellent nutty travel snacks gozinaki and churchkhela. Walnuts are used so inventively too, with the membranes used to flavour chacha and unripe ones preserved as jam. To walk past walnut trees was to think of the Georgian table.

Finally, we came to the Skhalta Monastery itself. Cows grazed freely by the 13th-century church and the smaller chapel, even older, with its medieval cellar for wine. Inside, a priest was talking to a group of children but as soon as he spotted us, he cut them short and came to greet us. I felt a stab of guilt. In English, he offered an explanation first about the history of the monastery (nobody can accurately date it as it is so old), then the church (how it had once been used as a mosque), before leading the way to a series of curious boxes, set in a dark corner, that appeared to be holding bones. Collected nearby, they were human, the remains of people who'd not had a proper burial. The macabre painting above them, he went on, of severed heads floating in a river running red, represented Georgians who had refused to convert to Islam.

The bones were eerie. I took photographs of them and later, when I went to look, I noticed that, while every other photograph of the interior was clear and in focus, all of the images of the bones were not. They looked as though they'd been taken from a moving car. There was no way to tell what they were.

Before returning to Batumi, we drove to Ghorjomi Mosque, the largest in the region and one of the furthest to the east. It was coming up for lunchtime and the village of greater Ghorjomi (population: 2,813), centred around the mosque and the Ghorjomi Youth Organisation building, was busy. It felt good to be on horizontal ground again as to get there we'd driven on terrifyingly vertical tracks. Dozens of village men, busy polluting the air with thick tobacco smoke, were sat hunched in conversation on shaded wooden benches. We offered a confusion of multilingual greetings and a friendly man named Mika stood up to lead us into the five-domed mosque, its minaret studded with speakers. I quickly consulted the catalogue and learned it had been completed in 1902, renovated in 1989, and was originally beautified by the paintings of Omer Usta and Usta Bin Ahmed, both Laz.

Inside, we were first met by a striking wall painting of an Ottoman steamship, then double-height columns, chandeliers and a carnival of colours dominated by emerald green, a favourite colour of Prophet Muhammad. There was so much to take in: the perfectly hoovered crimson carpets, a minbar almost psychedelic in its swirling colours, striped hallway ceilings, tesbih beads in a rainbow assortment, spare knitted skullcaps, framed white Arabic script. It was clearly a well-loved, and well-used mosque. Pride of the village.

James went outside with Mika, and as I stood there, alone in the stillness musing upon it all, I felt relief, and then something else. A pleasingly familiar feeling of being in between. I'd encountered a similar sensation at the Agara Mosque, where we'd stopped as well, with its harlequin painted walls and stencilled-on palm trees, a reference to the coast not so far away. It was a sensitivity, or mood, that rises up when between the Christian and Muslim worlds, rural hardship and great spiritual wealth, traditional isolation and modern interconnectedness, the authentic and the ersatz. Of being close, once again, to the Black Sea.

# Courgettes with Georgian Spices and Walnuts

A handy recipe for putting to use Georgian spices. Serve alongside salads and bread as part of a wider meze spread.

**SERVES 4**

1 tbsp olive oil, plus extra for drizzling

1 onion, finely chopped

3 large garlic cloves, thinly sliced

80g/2¾oz walnuts, toasted and broken into pieces

100g/3½oz sundried tomatoes

1 tbsp khmeli suneli (a mix of coriander seed, dried marigold petals, chilli pepper and blue fenugreek; if you don't have khmeli suneli then make a spice mix combining at least the chilli and the coriander seed)

½ tsp sweet paprika

3 courgettes (zucchini), cut into 1cm/½in diagonal slices

Sea salt flakes and freshly ground black pepper

70g/2½oz feta, crumbled

Handful of fresh summer herbs (a mixture of coriander (cilantro), parsley, mint, tarragon, dill), chopped

Line a large roasting tray with foil that will accommodate the courgettes in a single layer and preheat the oven to 180°C/350°F/gas mark 4.

Heat the oil in a frying pan and cook the onion until soft and starting to colour, then add the garlic and cook for another minute or so. Remove to a bowl. Combine the walnuts, sundried tomatoes and spices, then combine with the onion mixture.

Arrange the courgette slices in a single layer on the lined tray, then cover thickly with the nutty, spicy tomato mixture, drizzle with oil and sprinkle with salt and pepper. Roast for around 25–30 minutes, gently stirring the topping halfway through and, if it's looking a bit dry, drizzle over a little more oil. Serve garnished with crumbled feta and the fresh herbs.

# Pumpkin Soup with Barberries

In Georgia, soup is often gently spiced and topped with nuts and seeds, providing different textures. Barberries here add a welcome sour note while pumpkin seeds offer some crunch.

**SERVES 6**

2 tbsp olive oil, plus extra for drizzling

2 onions, finely chopped

Sea salt and freshly ground black pepper

Pinch of Svan salt (optional; see page 248 for homemade)

1kg/2lb 4oz pumpkin or squash peeled, deseeded and chopped into chunks

800ml/3½ cups chicken stock

150ml/scant ⅔ cup double (heavy) cream

Nutmeg for grating

Handful of pumpkin seeds and dried barberries or unsweetened dried cranberries

½ lemon, juiced

Heat the oil in a large, lidded saucepan or casserole and gently cook the onions, sprinkling over a little salt and pepper as you go (if you have some Svan salt a pinch here is a nice addition), until soft but not coloured. Add the pumpkin (or squash) and cook gently for 10 minutes, stirring occasionally to make sure nothing sticks to the bottom, until it starts to soften a bit. Season well.

Pour the stock into the pan, bring to the boil, then simmer, with the lid on, until the pumpkin or squash is very soft, 20 minutes at least depending on the size of your pieces.

Next, pour the cream into the pan, stir through well, then purée with a stick blender until entirely smooth, check the seasoning. Grate over a little nutmeg and stir in.

When ready to serve, toast the pumpkin seeds in a dry frying pan, then scatter over the bowls of soup along with the barberries. Drizzle over a little more olive oil and a squeeze of lemon.

"The dishes and cups he used to create art were worn as they were broken but in his hands they were transformed. Damaged things, that people forget, that they throw away, he gave them new meaning. Transformation was very important to him." Arshit Mikayelyan, Curator of the Parajanov Museum

# EPILOGUE

The mournful sound of the duduk, a double reed woodwind instrument, droned out from speakers, spreading across central Yerevan in the hot mid-afternoon. I stopped, recognising what sounded like music from the film *Gladiator*. Loud and hypnotic, it drew me in like a forcefield towards the grand Opera and Ballet Theatre from where it was coming. Outside, men smoked cigarettes while being interviewed by local news reporters who were jostling each other with fuzzy microphones. Above the door hung a clue: a portrait of Djivan Gasparyan, one of Armenia's greatest musicians.

Gasparyan had died in America in July 2021, aged 92, and his body had been returned to Armenia to be laid to rest at the grand Komitas Pantheon, beside other great artists we've met in this book: Sergei Parajanov, Mariam Aslamazyan, Aram Khachaturian, Alexander Tamanian, Martiros Saryan, and Komitas himself. Now, hundreds of fans and friends were arriving at the opera house, a venue both grand enough and large enough for such an occasion, to pay their final respects.

I stepped into the busy hall. Sitting closest to the coffin, topped with huge sprays of yellow and white roses, were women in black who fanned themselves and shook the hands of those queuing to express sympathy. In Armenia, Gasparyan had been awarded the title of People's Artist, the Knight of the Order of the First Degree, as well as the Order of Mesrop Mashtots for services to the homeland. The stirring music played on, and suddenly it seemed that, even without this solemn occasion, it would be the most funereal music in the world. And it struck me that while similar instruments are played in the Balkans and elsewhere, this particular duduk music could only have come from Armenia, where such melodies feature in manuscripts as old as the Middle Ages, and where the instruments are still carved from superior local apricot wood.

I watched the candles beside the coffin flicker a bit longer and then walked away, for a final lunch of Armenian salads, lavash and madzoon, my heart a little heavy. There is much melancholy in Armenia, but it is matched by creativity, spirituality, strength and wonder and this sorrowful gathering that I had stumbled upon seemed a perfect reminder of all that.

## A BATTLE OF THE BLACK SEA

I could never have imagined, when I set out to write the first in this trilogy, *Black Sea*, over ten years ago, what would happen between then and now. Back then, I had written: 'The Black Sea, overflowing with intrigue, often feels as though it is the pivot of the geopolitical world' and since Russia's diabolical full-scale invasion of Ukraine began, those words ring even more true.

Countless news reports have focused on the Black Sea since the invasion began. The sinking of the *Moskva* (the flagship of Russia's Black Sea Fleet), the massive grain-smuggling operations taking place on ships and at ports, political wrangling over Putin's warships on the Bosphorus, Russian ships launching cruise missiles at Ukrainian cities and humanitarian corridors through the Black Sea for getting grain safely out. Sea drones in the air, chains of mines below the waters. Rumours circulated about Russia potentially building a shipyard on the coast in Abkhazia, Georgia's breakaway region. This war, in some ways, is a battle of the Black Sea.

Georgia and Armenia have been directly affected and not only because tens of thousands of fleeing Russians have arrived in their cities. Armenia feels let down by Russia, its long-term ally, which largely stood aside as Nagorno-Karabakh was taken by Azerbaijan. In Georgia, a country polarised politically, hundreds of men left to fight in Ukraine with Kyiv's forces, many belonging to the Georgian Legion, formed in 2014 during fighting in the Donbas region and when the Kremlin illegally annexed Crimea. And, more generally, there is a fear that Georgia is not secure.

Central Asia, too, the vast former-Soviet region covered in *Red Sands*, the second book in this trilogy, has been impacted as well. Businesses have been trying to diversify their trade relationships and to establish transit routes that bypass Russia, and families fear for relatives working in Moscow and Siberia who may be recruited to fight in Ukraine. All of this was present as James and I walked through Armenia and Georgia, not least as sometimes he was filing stories to a newspaper desk in London about Russia's manoeuvres and warmongering while we were on the road.

## MOUNTAINS, KITCHENS, ARTISTS

Many of the journeys, places and encounters reported here defied all expectations and consequently refuse to be forgotten now months, even years, on. I had no idea, for example, how singular Svan culture is or how intense the demonic summer storms are in Armenia, or how unexpected encounters would present themselves with fruit-pickers, priests and polyphonic singers.

The word constellation kept coming to mind as that is how the journeys often felt, like a sky full of stars where you could hop from one to the next and to the next, and by stepping forward, a multiple exposure of different worlds would start to form. There was often a sense of being sidetracked and sidetracked again. And that, of course, is the joy of travel and the joy of walking when only the day itself matters.

Characteristic differences were found too, naturally enough, across both landscapes and kitchens. There were meals so distinctive, by place, time and taste, that they could never be repeated: the plump little trout served at the Writers' House on Lake Sevan, and the gata the next morning as the waters glittered; the traditional Russian-style lunch shared with the Molokan villagers; and the Svan kubdari eaten at the Lamproba festival in the snow.

There were also cultural unknowns that helped to stitch together history and context. I knew Parajanov's films, but the remarkable sisters Mariam and Yeranuhi Aslamazyan were entirely new to me. Their paintings not only underlined Armenian culture but also what they had to do in order to work and create under the Soviet system. The Armenian painter Martiros Saryan was an artist so skilled and so unique that he ought to be as well known as his contemporaries Mark Rothko and Pablo Picasso (who all died within three years of one another). He wasn't just one of the best painters of Armenia in the 20th century, so masterfully depicting fruit, the countryside and holy Mount Ararat, he was one of the finest artists anywhere of that century.

Books, written in English that I had at my disposal in libraries and online, of alpinists were, predictably, overwhelmingly male, European and upper-class. But by spending time in Georgia, I became transfixed by the stories, and photographs, of the great Georgian climbers, namely Guram Tikanadze and Mikhail Khergiani, picking up what I could from exhibitions, websites and their museums in mountainous Svaneti. There are many more whose stories ought to be told, too, more often, and in far greater detail. The climber Joyce Dunsheath, a modest perfectionist with a skill for diplomacy, was another writer whose work became known to me only during my research. It is the thinnest of lines that separates confidence from arrogance, and I think Dunsheath stayed on the right side of things.

## MAGIC GATHERED, STEP BY STEP

Armenia and Georgia are well known to travellers for three things in particular: food, mountains and hospitality. Therefore it seemed to me to be entirely natural to conclude this colour trilogy with a series of walks in these two countries, through the lands between the Black and Caspian seas.

Sometimes the walks felt like a response to Russia's war against Ukraine. A way to process such fast-moving and terrible events, and a desperate need to be reminded of nature, of normal days spent in the hills. But more broadly, stepping forward into the valleys and cities, mountains and flatlands of Armenia and Georgia, in all weathers, was a general reply to the modern world with its megacities and endless demands on our attention and time. Walking forces you to consider the moment, to look away from the screen. I found myself continually sustained, and surprised, mentally and physically, so much so that I would recommend walking in the South Caucasus to anyone able to do it.

'Since man cannot live without miracles, he will provide himself with miracles of his own making,' wrote Fyodor Dostoevsky in *The Brothers Karamazov*. And while I think Dostoevsky was writing with sorcery in mind, his words can be well applied to the simple magic that is pulling on a pair of boots, heading out of the door and going for a walk.

# RECOMMENDED READING

A concise guide to some of the books and resources I have found helpful, by no means comprehensive.

## ARMENIA – BOOKS

Abrahamian, Levon and Sweezy, Nancy (eds), *Armenian Folk Arts, Culture, and Identity* (Indiana University Press, 2001)

Chaubin, Frédéric, *Cosmic Communist Constructions* (Taschen, 2022)

Grossman, Vasily (trans. Robert and Elizabeth Chandler), *An Armenian Sketchbook* (MacLehose Press, 2014)

Harutyunian, Tigran, *Yerevan: Architectural Guide* (DOM Publishers, 2017)

Herwig, Christopher, *Soviet Bus Stops* (FUEL, 2015)

Leahy, Kate et al. *Lavash* (Chronicle Books, 2019)

Mandelstam, Osip (trans. Sidney Monas), *Journey to Armenia* (Notting Hill Editions, 2011)

Marsden, Philip, *The Crossing Place* (William Collins, 2015)

Walker, Christopher (ed.), *Visions of Ararat: Writings on Armenia* (I.B. Tauris, 2005)


## GEORGIA – BOOKS

Aleksidze, Nikoloz, *Georgia – A Cultural Journey Through the Wardrop Collection* (Bodleian Library Publishing, 2018)

Anderson, Tony, *Bread and Ashes: A Walk through the Mountains of Georgia* (Vintage, 2004)

Baerug, Richard, *The Essence of the Caucasus: Svaneti* (MTA, 2019)

Baumer, Christopher, *History of the Caucasus Vol. 1: At the Crossroads of Empires* (I.B. Tauris, 2021)

Blanch, Lesley, *The Sabres of Paradise* (Carroll & Graf, 1995, first published 1960)

Bullough, Oliver, *Let Our Fame be Great: Journeys among the Defiant People of the Caucasus* (Penguin, 2010)

Burford, Tim, *Georgia* (Bradt Travel Guides, 2008)

Capalbo, Carla, *Tasting Georgia: A Food and Wine Journey in the Caucasus* (Pallas Athene, 2017)

Chiladze, Otar, *A Man Was Going Down the Road* (Garnett Press, 2012)

de Waal, Thomas, *The Caucasus: An Introduction* (OUP, 2010)

Dumas, Alexandre, *Adventures in Caucasia* (Chilton Books, 1962)

Freshfield, Douglas, *Travels in the Central Caucasus and Bashan* (Longmans, Green, & Co., 1869)

Goldstein, Darra, *The Georgian Feast: The Vibrant Culture and Savory Food of the Republic of Georgia* (University of California Press, 1999, first published HarperCollins, 1993)

Hercules, Olia, *Kaukasis the Cookbook: A Culinary Journey through Georgia, Azerbaijan & Beyond* (Octopus, 2017)

King, Charles, *The Black Sea: A History* (OUP, 2004)

Marsden, Philip, *The Spirit-Wrestlers: A Russian Journey* (HarperCollins, 1998)

Nasmyth, Peter, *Georgia: In the Mountains of Poetry* (Duckworth, 2017, first published Curzon, 1998)

Rayfield, Donald, *The Literature of Georgia: A History* (Routledge, 2020, first published Clarendon Press, 1994)

Rustaveli, Shota (trans. Wardrop, Marjory), *The Man in the Panther's Skin: A Romantic Epic* (Royal Asiatic Society, 1912)

Saldadze, Anna, *Untamed: 8000 Vintages of Georgian Wine* (Sulakauri, 2018)

Steavenson, Wendell, *Stories I Stole* (Atlantic, 2002)

Steinbeck, John, *A Russian Journal* (Heinemann, 1949)

Tuskadze, Tiko, *Supra: A Feast of Georgian Cooking* (Pavilion Books, 2017)

Wheeler, Angela, *Tbilisi: Architectural Guide* (DOM Publishers, 2023)

**SOURCES AND BOOKS CONSULTED**

Research for *Green Mountains* has combined books, newspapers, journals and websites.

**ARMENIA**

**Trouble in the Valley of Woes**

Vayots Dzor Region. armgeo.am/en/vayots_dzor/

This Shoe Had Prada Beat by 5,500 Years nytimes.com/2010/06/10/science/10shoe.html

Red Fox. linkedin.com/company/red-fox-north-america https://us.redfoxoutdoor.com/pages/about-our-founders

Vayots Dzor Check List. inaturalist.ca/check_lists/13205-Vayots-Dzor-Check-List

Advice to future TCTers. valismaili.org/advice-to-future-tcters#Wildlife%20strategy

**The golden way to Noravank**

Noravank Monastery: sites.courtauld.ac.uk/crossingfrontiers/crossing-frontiers/armenia/noravank-monastery/

Allen, Tom and Holding, Deirdre, *Armenia* (Bradt Travel Guides, 2018)

Ford, Adam, *The Art of Mindful Walking* (Ivy Press, 2012)

Macaulay, Rose, *Personal Pleasures* (Ecco Press, 1990)

**Diving into the aquatic alchemy of Jermuk**

Armenian Bottled Water Banned In U.S. azatutyun.am/a/1587090.html

Water as a landmark of Armenia armgeo.am/en/water-in-armenia

Environmental impact of bottled water 'up to 3,500 times greater than tap water' theguardian.com/environment/2021/aug/05/environmental-impact-of-bottled-water-up-to-3500-times-greater-than-tap-water

Jermuk water recalled over arsenic level dailynews.com/2007/03/09/jermuk-water-recalled-over-arsenic-level/

A tale of arsenic and old ways latimes.com/archives/la-xpm-2007-apr-02-me-armenia2-story.html

**Roving through Yerevan and the history of the new**

Harutyunian, Tigran, *Yerevan: Architectural Guide* (DOM Publishers, 2017)

Urban streams: countrylife.co.uk/architecture/urban-streams-the-forgotten-history-of-britains-drinking-fountains-246355

Where Are Our Manuscripts? evnreport.com/raw-unfiltered/where-are-our-manuscripts-stories-of-loss-and-survival/

Salt: armgeo.am/en/armenian-salt/

Sweezy, Nancy and Abrahmiam, Levon (ed.) *Armenian Folk Arts, Culture and Identity* (Indiana University Press, 2001)

Avo Uvezian: cigaraficionado.com/article/avo-uvezian-the-man-in-the-white-suit-7486

Khachaturian, a Leading Soviet Composer, Dies at 74 nytimes.com/1978/05/03/archives/khachaturian-a-leading-soviet-composer-dies-at-74-works-included.html

Walker, Christopher (ed.), *Visions of Ararat: Writings on Armenia* (I.B. Tauris, 2005)

**The light in which we walk: dinner with Father Sahak Martirosyan**

Martirosyan, Sahak, *Native Land and Churches Through the Eyes of a Priest* (Antares, 2019)

**Black caviar and smashed plates – meandering through Parajanov's mind**

Steffen, James, 'Parajanov's Playful Poetics', *Journal of Film and Video* (University of Illinois Press, Winter 1995–96)

*The Colour of Pomegranates* theguardian.com/film/2014/oct/07/the-colour-of-pomegranates-sergei-parajanov-london-film-festival-2014

Life History of a Fruit eefb.org/retrospectives/symbol-and-tradition-in-parajanovs-caucasian-trilogy

About the museum: parajanovmuseum.am/about-museum

The darkness before the dawn theguardian.com/film/1999/nov/26/culture.features

Sergei Parajanov's kaleidoscopic shadow klassiki.online/the-kaleidoscopic-shadow-of-sergei-parajanov

**A dining room at the Writers' House**

Guesthouse of the Armenian Writers' Union: architectuul.com/architecture/guesthouse-of-the-armenian-writers-union

Lake Sevan Writers' Resort: new-east-archive.org/articles/show/9184/lake-sevan-writers-resort-history-armenia-modernist-masterpiece

Gata atlasobscura.com/foods/gata-cake-geghard-monastery

Gata seriouseats.com/gata-5185123

Mandelstam, Osip, *Journey to Armenia* (Notting Hill Editions, 2011)

**Pilgrimage to a marble monastery**

Komitas Vardapet: theguardian.com/music/2011/apr/21/komitas-vardapet-folk-music-armenia

Marmashen Monastery: sites.courtauld.ac.uk/crossingfrontiers/crossing-frontiers/armenia/marmashen-monastery/

Adamian, Martin S. and Klem, Jr, Daniel, *A Field Guide to Birds of Armenia* (American University of Armenia, 1997)

## The dynamic abundance of the Aslamazyan sisters

The Armenian Frida Kahlo: mirrorspectator.com/2018/08/17/the-armenian-frida-kahlo-on-mariam-aslamazyans-110th-anniversary

Beloved Artists of the Soviet Union: evnreport.com/arts-and-culture/mariam-and-eranuhi-aslamazyan-beloved-artists-of-the-soviet-union

## We are wanderers, we are lost

Bardzrakash St Gregory Monastery: wmf.org/project/bardzrakash-st-gregory-monastery

Forest Insect and Disease Management in Armenia: fs.usda.gov/Internet/FSE_DOCUMENTS/fsbdev2_026413.pdf

Hovhannes Tumanyan: armeniapedia.org/wiki/Hovhannes_Tumanyan

## Lunch with the milk drinkers

Molokans in Armenia: jam-news.net/molokans-in-armenia-20-years-ago-and-now/

## A one-mile radius to taste Tbilisi

Cradle of lettuce: eurasianet.org/new-study-adds-to-caucasus-brag-sheet-cradle-of-lettuce

Russians in Georgia: https://eurasianet.org/russian-influx-boosts-georgian-economy-but-not-everyone-is-feeling-the-boom]

Matsun, Matsoni: https://eurasianet.org/armenia-georgia-battle-over-yogurt

Wheeler, Angela, *Tbilisi: Architectural Guide* (DOM Publishers, 2023)

Tbilisi history: https://www.advantour.com/georgia/tbilisi/history.htm

## Mandarins in the snow

Mount Ushba: summitpost.org/mount-ushba/153969

Freshfield, Douglas, *The Exploration of the Caucasus* (2 vols, E. Arnold, 1869, 1902)

Freshfield, Douglas, *Travels in the Central Caucasus and Bashan: Including Visits to Ararat and Tabreez and Ascents of Kazbek and Elbruz* (Longmans, Green, & Co., 1869)

Vittorio Sella: https://www.fondazionesella.org/photo-funds/sella-vittorio-5/

Bamberger, Benjamin, dissertation: 'Mountains of Discontent' (University of Illinois, 2019)

Dunsheath, Joyce, 'Climbing in The Caucasus Mountains of The U.S.S.R. 1957.' An original article from the *Geographical Journal*, 1958.

Dunsheath, Joyce, *Guest of the Soviets: Moscow and the Caucasus 1957* (Constable and Co., 1959)

Svan towers: heritagedaily.com/2021/05/the-svan-blood-revenge-towers/139210

Cryptocurrency: eurasianet.org/georgias-mountainous-cryptocurrency-problem

*Salt for Svanetia*: theguardian.com/film/2022/sep/26/salt-for-svanetia-review-communism-medieval-georgia-mikhail-kalatozov

In Memoriam: https://www.alpinejournal.org.uk/Contents/Contents_1979_files/AJ 1979 265-271 In Memoriam.pdf

### Wandering among the dead: meat pies and burning birch

Vakhtang Pilpani: https://bankwatch.org/svaneti/people/vakhtang-pilpani

Strabo: perseus.tufts.edu/hopper/text?doc=urn:cts:greeklit:tlg0099.tlg001.perseus-eng2:11.2.19

### Mountain tigers and dazzling alpinists

Khergiani: georgia.travel/mikheil-khergiani-house-museum

Svaneti Historical Ethnographical Museum: georgianmuseums.ge/en/museum/georgian-national-museum-svaneti-museum/

Guram Tikanadze: /kolga.ge/exhibitions/guram-tikanadze-1

Guram Tikanadze: cartveli.com/guram-tikanadze-the-other-soviet-man.php

### Strolling summertime Svaneti: old gold and alpine flowers

Baerug, Richard, *The Essence of the Caucasus: Svaneti* (MTA, 2019)

Baumer, Christoph, *History of the Caucasus Vol. 1: At the Crossroads of Empires* (I.B. Tauris, 2021)

Strabo: perseus.tufts.edu/hopper/text?doc=Perseus:text:1999.01.0239:book=11

### The magnetism of Mount Kazbek

Freshfield, Douglas, *The Exploration of the Caucasus* (2 vols, E. Arnold, 1902)

**Rambling through the colours of Truso Gorge**

Borjomi: rferl.org/a/georgia-borjomi-water-production-dispute/31895762.html

Borjomi: oc-media.org/borjomi-ceases-production-citing-ukraine-war/

In Living Color: rferl.org/a/georgia-color-photographs-sergei-prokudin-gorsky-russian-photographer/31047349.html

Transcaucasian Trail: transcaucasiantrail.org/en/home/

**Hill songs and deadly moonshine**

Marjory Wardrop and Guria: kartvelologi.tsu.ge/public/en/arqive/19/10

Marjory Wardrop: treasures.bodleian.ox.ac.uk/treasures/marjory-wardrop/

Rustaveli, Shota (trans. Wardrop, Marjory), *The Man in the Panther's Skin: A Romantic Epic* (Royal Asiatic Society, 1912)

Varlam Simonishvili: georgian-music.com/free_music/029.php

**By foot along Georgia's tea route**

Tea: rferl.org/a/the-revival-of-georgias-tea-industry/30230293.html

Why did the Georgian tea industry collapse? renegadetea.com/blogs/renegade-rumblings/why-did-the-georgian-tea-industry-collapse

Brothers Nobel Batumi Technological Museum: georgianmuseums.ge/en/museum/brothers-nobel-batumi-technology-museum/

**Promenading the Black Sea's green cape**

Steinbeck, John *A Russian Journal* (Penguin Classics, 1999, 1st edition Heinemann, 1949)

Batumi Botanical Garden: bbg.ge/en/home

**Walking from mosque to monastery**

Wooden mosques of Adjara: indigenousoutsiders.com

**EPILOGUE**

Djivan Gasparyan: news.am/eng/news/655127.html

John Muir: theguardian.com/environment/2020/jul/23/john-muir-sierra-club-apologizes-for-racist-views

# ACKNOWLEDGEMENTS

Thank you firstly to my husband, James Kilner, there is nobody I would rather walk with.

Enormous and heartfelt thanks to the exceptional publishing team at Quadrille who have worked so brilliantly and so tirelessly with me not only on *Green Mountains* but the other books in this trilogy – it's been a long and winding road. Thank you to Sarah Lavelle, Ruth Tewkesbury, Dave Brown, Theodore Kaye, Stacey Cleworth, Katherine Case, Liz Boyd, Ola O. Smit, Holly Cowgill, Lu Cottle, Martyna Wlodarska, Pip Spence, Tamsin English, Stephanie Evans, Claire Rochford, Amy Stephenson, Ivana Zorn and Tabitha Hawkins. Special thanks to Sofie Shearman for working closely and sympathetically with me on this particular book. I am also grateful to my friend and kitchen whizz Giverny Tattersfield, who has helped me with the recipe testing throughout.

Many thanks to my agent, Jessica Woollard at DHA, ably assisted by Esme Bright, who has been with me every step of the way with invaluable advice and inspiration.

To my wonderful friends and colleagues who share my love for Georgia and Armenia: Howard Amos, Amelia Stewart, Nadia Beard, Meagan Neal, Joshua Kucera, Neil Hauer, Luba Balyan, Hans Gutbrod, Will Dunbar, Paul Rimple, Justyna Mielnikiewicz, Nino Oniani, Tom Pinnegar, Timothy Merkel, Masho Bojgua – thank you all. Thanks a million to Helen Stokes and Noriko Kumagai who've stuck with me for well over two decades of friendship, your support means everything.

Thank you with all my heart to booksellers, book festival organisers and librarians everywhere. To my local bookshops, and those who have so kindly supported my books over the years, I appreciate all you do and I honestly don't know where I'd be without the general goodness of bookshops. Golden Hare Books, Topping & Company Booksellers, The White Horse Bookshop, The Portobello Bookshop, Daunt Books, Stanfords, Pushkin House and John Sandoe Books - thank you. In the USA, thanks in particular to Kitchen Arts & Letters, Harvard Book Store, Omnivore Books, Book Larder, Archestratus Books and Now Serving. Also, my sincere gratitude to the generous team at Geo Café in Caversham, run by Keti Maglakelidze, who offer Georgian hospitality and flavours to the community I grew up in. I hope to see you all soon.

It was a privilege to spend time in Armenia and Georgia in order to write and research this book. My greatest thanks of all goes out to the cooks, drivers, tea makers, hoteliers and the serving staff of these two remarkable countries. This book is for them and for walkers everywhere who find peace on the hills.

# INDEX

Caroline Eden is a writer contributing to the travel, food and arts pages of *the Guardian*, the *Financial Times* and *The Times Literary Supplement*.

She is the author of several books including *Samarkand: Recipes & Stories from Central Asia & the Caucasus* (2016), *Black Sea: Dispatches and Recipes Through Darkness and Light* (2018), *Red Sands: Reportage and Recipes through Central Asia* (2020) and *Cold Kitchen* (2024).

Her books have been reviewed widely and have won many awards including the prestigious Art of Eating Prize and the André Simon Award. *Green Mountains: Walking the Caucasus with Recipes*, following on from *Black Sea* and *Red Sands*, concludes her epic 'colour trilogy', spanning from Eastern Europe to Central Asia.

She lives in Edinburgh.

Twitter and Instagram: @edentravels